ALLAH CALLS FOR PEACE

Bridging Religions

Sylvain Romain

TEACH Services, Inc.
PUBLISHING
www.TEACHServices.com • (800) 367-1844

Published in Calhoun, Georgia, USA
ISBN-13: 978-1-4796-1880-4 (Paperback)
ISBN-13: 978-1-4796-1881-1 (ePub)
Library of Congress Control Number: 2025919039

All scripture references are the author's own translations from the original languages (Arabic, Greek, and Hebrew).

The website references in this book have been shortened using a URL shortener and redirect service called 1ref.us, which TEACH Services manages. If you find that a reference no longer works, please contact us and let us know which one is not working so that we can correct it. Any personal website addresses that the author included are managed by the author. TEACH Services is not responsible for the accuracy or permanency of any links.

For more information, visit www.HopeToShare.org.
To contact the author, email info@HopeToShare.org.

Published by

TEACH Services, Inc.
PUBLISHING
www.TEACHServices.com • (800) 367-1844

About the Cover

The dove on the front cover is calligraphy specially designed by my Sahrawi friend Mohamed Sulaiman Labat. The text is a quote from the Honored Quran, Surah Al-Fatḥ 48:4:

هُوَ الَّذِي أَنزَلَ السَّكِينَةَ فِي قُلُوبِ الْمُؤْمِنِينَ لِيَزْدَادُوا إِيمَانًا مَّعَ إِيمَانِهِمْ
وَلِلَّهِ جُنُودُ السَّمَاوَاتِ وَالْأَرْضِ وَكَانَ اللَّهُ عَلِيمًا حَكِيمًا

> He is the One who sent down peace into the hearts of the believers, that they may grow in faith. To Allah belong the powers of heaven and earth. Allah is full of knowledge and wisdom.

DEDICATION

I have written this book as a Christian and dedicate it to my Muslim brothers and sisters. Yet readers of all faiths will benefit from its content, as it will help each one discover some overlooked connections between monotheistic religions. If this book clears a few stumbling blocks, it will have served its purpose—*al-ḥamdu lillahi* (for the glory of God alone).

–Sylvain Romain, PhD

بسم الله الرحمن الرحيم

Table of Contents

A WORD TO THE READER Food for Thought viii

PREFACE A Personal Appeal to the Reader: To Stone, or to Remove Stones? ix
What About Religious Conflicts? x
A Call for a Breach in the Wall xi
Some Verses from the Honored Bible Related to the Preface 13

TERMINOLOGY 15

CHAPTER 1 The Quranic View on Christian Apostasy 19
The Odyssey of Christianity 20
Pagan Elements 22
The Rise of the West Roman Church 23
Theological Implications 24
Apostasy Today? 26
Al-kāfirūn (The Concealers) 26
Only *Some* of Them 27
They Are Not All Alike 28
Muhammad (pbuh) and His Followers' Attention to Christianity 31
Christians Persecuted by "Christians" 33
Christians Protected by Muslims 34
The Ottoman Empire 35
Back to the Roots of Islam 37
An Important Remark and a Cordial Invitation 39
Some Verses from the Honored Bible Related to Chapter 1 41
The Concept of *Islām* in the Honored Bible 41
Apostasy Foretold 41
Not All Christians are Apostates 42

CHAPTER 2 The Honored Injil—A Corrupted Book? 43
The Testimony of the Honored Quran 44
The Meaning of *Ḥarrafa* 46
The "Notarization" of the Honored Bible 48

The Contribution of Archaeology 50
More Reasons to Doubt? 51
Theological Divergences between the Sacred Books 52
Hudan: A Guidance to Mankind 53
Conclusion of Chapter 2 54
Some Verses from the Honored Bible Related to Chapter 2 57

CHAPTER 3 The Blessed Feast Eid al-Adha 59
A Shocking Command 59
Submission Implies Obedience 61
Divine Intervention 62
The Meaning 63
A Matter of Life and Death 64
How It All Began 65
What Is Sin? 68
What Is Death? 69
A Worldwide Pandemic 70
Good News Ahead! 72
Taqwāh 73
Two Brothers—Two Choices 74
Divine Guidance 76
Some Verses from the Honored Bible Related to Chapter 3 79
The Sacrifice of Ibrahim's (pbuh) Son 79
The Fall of Adam and Eve (pbut) 80
The Cloth of Righteousness 81

CHAPTER 4 Allah Will Give Peace 83
Who Will Set Us Free? 84
Who Paid the Ransom? 85
Will Allah Forgive? 86
A Cry for Mercy 88
The Right Way 90
Some Verses from the Honored Bible Related to Chapter 4 91
Not a Single Act of Goodness Can Bring Us Closer to Allah 91
Taqwāh and the "Lamb Coming from Allah" 91

CHAPTER 5 Does Allah Have a Son? The Truth about Al-Masih Isa ibn Maryam (piuh) 93
The Oneness of the Christian God 95
The Meaning of "Son of Allah" 96
Ibn Maryam (The Son of Mary) 99
Rasūl Ullah (Allah's Messenger) 99
Rūḥ min-hu (Spirit Coming from Him) 100
Al-Masih (The Messiah) 101
Al-Masih (piuh) Purifies and Heals 101
Isa (Jesus (piuh)) 102
Kalimat Ullah (Allah's Word) 102
Wajīh wa muqarrab (Glorious and Near to Allah) 103
Ayāh lil-'ālamīn (A Sign for the Worlds) 104
Who Is *Raḥmat min-nā* (A Mercy from Us) 105
The Good News of a Mercy 107
Az-zakī (The Pure One) 107
Mubārak (Blessed) 108
Qaul al-ḥaqq (The Expression of the Truth) 108
The Deeds of Al-Masih Isa ibn Maryam (piuh) 109
Who Al-Masih Isa ibn Maryam (piuh) Really Is 111
An Apparent Contradiction 112
The One Who Says: "Follow Me!" and "Obey Me!" 113
Conclusion of Chapter 5 116
Some Verses from the Honored Bible Related to Chapter 5 117
What Jesus (piuh) Means to Us 117
What Jesus (piuh) Can Do 117
What Jesus (piuh) Has Promised 118
The Voluntary Humiliation of Jesus (piuh) 119
Also Consider 120

Closing Words 121

Bibliography 123

Other Works by the Author 125

A Word to the Reader

Food for Thought

The attentive reader will notice that some of the statements made in this book may diverge from the established interpretations of the Honored Quran, especially from those based on the Tafsīr and the Sunnah.

It would have been easy for the author to reproduce what has been expressed so many times. However, he deliberately chose to venture into a different approach.

The reason is simple: The author wanted to look at the quranic message with new eyes, assuming that his non-Muslim education would help him unfold some unknown truths—if any.

The author's only motivation in sharing his discoveries and possibly offering new insights is to enrich your faith.

Therefore, this essay invites you to open your mind and look fresh at the Honored Quran.

Whenever the author's unconventional approach brings him to conclusions that differ from usual views, keep in mind that he only intends to seek mutual understanding by highlighting the common ground between the Honored Bible and the Honored Quran instead of the divergences.

Believing that his research deserves at least a look, the author thanks you for accepting his work as a sign of goodwill toward peace and reconciliation between religions.

As-salām^u 'alaykum wa raḥmat-Ullāh^i wa barakatuhu!

بسم الله الرحمن الرحيم

Preface

A Personal Appeal to the Reader: To Stone, or to Remove Stones?

As-salām[u] 'alaykum wa raḥmat-Ullāh[i] wa barakatuhu!

May the peace of Allah, His mercy and blessing, be upon all of us! That is my deepest wish, because peace has become a scarce commodity. If peace is defined as the absence of war, deterrence and protection become necessary. Thus it seems that Planet Earth has been invaded by a strange kind of enemy called "the protective device." Walls and fences made of stones or of technological gadgets can be found worldwide—as if they could keep dangers away by dividing people.

From the Great Wall of China to the Mexican border, walls summon admiration or horror. At the same time, their imposing size and the enormous amounts spent throughout the ages on these kinds of bastions create a feeling of awkwardness since, unlike other inventions, they must endure and resist for thousands of years.

Barriers are supposed to protect and, therefore, be insurmountable. Occasionally, someone may open a gap in one to fire some poisonous arrows at the enemy and then quickly retreat to his or her supposed security. That is the rule if you want to feel secure.

Soldiers on both sides of the intra-Korean demarcation line have been commanded never to look in each other's direction. Isn't it, to a certain extent, the same in human relationships?

"Beware of the dog" is written on a big sign, and a video camera is put in the corner of the yard, reassuring many that the threat lurking beyond their fence can thus be stopped.

All of this means that the barriers are mainly in our heads. The *Mauer* in Berlin divided the German nation for twenty-eight years. It was torn down more than a generation ago, but it took a long time to remove the rocky prejudices from Easterners' and Westerners' intellectual and emotional worlds. There is still a long way to go ....

What About Religious Conflicts?

More than ever, the world longs for unity. Many seek it in interfaith dialogue. However, religion seems to cause more division than harmony. Stepping into *terra incognita* (the unknown world) creates insecurity, and some believe that the best way to protect oneself is to convince dissenters of their own understanding of the truth. Indeed, haven't some of the saddest chapters of history been written with the blood of religious tensions?

As one example among others, contention between Christians and Muslims has been fueled by theological disputes that often end up in hatred and dogmatism. The Western world is in danger of sinking into "islamophobia," while many Muslims perceive Christianity to be the very root of evil. Where could the solution lie?

- Should we draw lines to separate the quarreling spiritual children of Ibrahim (pbuh) like wrestlers in a ring?
- Do we need more fences between synagogues, churches, and mosques, like those existing between countries and private properties?
- Or is it not time to realize that piling stones has brought mankind nowhere and will never bring it anywhere?
- Why not simply bury the hatchet and stand together?
- Let us get rid of the rubble of the past, and let us break down barricades!

If you think this way, you are on the same wavelength as me, the author of this book. In tireless dialogue between both religions, I have held seminars and lectures in sixty-nine countries, teaching in churches and mosques, schools and universities, while sitting among Muslim and Christian scholars. My ultimate goal is to identify the stumbling blocks and to reassemble them into bridges.

Dialogue implies the readiness to agree to disagree. Working toward interfaith understanding neither presupposes nor implicates the acceptance of another creed. This is why bridging is possible.

A safe way to consolidate one's prejudices is to avoid facing a glimpse of another reality. Yet opening up to the other side may reveal that it is not necessarily the place where badness resides. In fact, looking into the eyes of an imagined enemy might connect you with a brother or a sister who possibly has the same longing for harmony as you.

By the way, have you ever considered that most Christians who were born and raised in a Christian world would be Muslims if they were born and brought up in a Muslim home? In the same way, most Muslims born and raised in Muslim surroundings would be Christians if they were born and brought up in a Christian family!

This simple reflection demonstrates that neither nationality nor education makes you good or bad.

A Call for a Breach in the Wall

Dear fellow Christian and Muslim readers (or whatever your belief is), the book you have in your hands is a solemn call to break the vicious cycle that has been dividing religions for too many centuries.

As we all claim to be the spiritual descendants of the very same prophet Ibrahim (pbuh), let us stop banging our heads against the rocks, and let us open the gates, realizing that walls signify nothing but bankrupt efforts to resolve discord. Only the insecure need security measures; those who know where they stand can move forward courageously.

> “Those who know where they stand can move forward courageously”

Therefore, everyone who dares to think outside the box will be rewarded. It corresponds perfectly to what is written in the Honored Quran:

> Al-Baqarah 2:112
> 112 Who submits to Allah and practices goodness has a reward waiting with his Lord. There will be no fear nor grief for him.

In this book, I will try to give answers to some misunderstandings regarding Islam and Christianity:

- Are Christians as wicked as some think?
- Are they all the same?
- Do Christians worship three gods?
- Which parts of the Honored Bible have been corrupted?
- Does the God of the Christians have a son?

May my passionate vision fill you with the desire to know more about Allah the Glorious as the supreme Source of perfect harmony!

As soon as you find peace of mind in Him, share it with those beyond the barrier: an enemy, a family member, or the believer of another faith.

Let us join hands and remove the wall! Let us break the stumbling blocks and find the precious gems in them! It may take some time, and both sides need patience. But then the sight of diamonds shining in a dark world should be worth the effort.

Are you ready? Let's get started!

Sylvain Romain

Some Verses from the Honored Bible

Related to the Preface

Taurat, Solomon's Proverbs 12:20[1]

20 Those who have deceitful intentions keep silent, but those who promote peace are full of joy.

Taurat, Solomon's Proverbs 17:1

1 Better a dry piece of bread with peace of mind than a feasting house with strife.

Taurat, Isaiah 58:6

6 Isn't this the type of fast I've chosen? Free the chains of injustice and untie the cords of servitude, liberate the oppressed, and break every form of bondage!

Taurat, Jeremiah 29:11

11 The Lord says, "I know what my thoughts are toward you, thoughts of peace and not of misfortune. My desire is to give you a future and hope."

Zabur, Psalm 18:30

30 With my God, I can jump over walls.

Injil, Gospel of Matthew 5:9

9 Blessed are those who work for peace. For they will be called "sons of God."

Injil, Gospel of Matthew 5:23, 24

23 If you present your offering at the altar and there, and it occurs that your brother has something against you,

1 The Book of Proverbs, Chapter 12, Verse 20

[24] Leave your offering there in front of the altar! Go and talk to him first, then come and present your offering.

Injil, Gospel of Luke 10:5, 6

[5] When you enter a house, say, "Peace to this house!"

[6] If anyone there is a son of peace, your peace will rest on him; if not, it will return to you.

Injil, Epistle of Paul to the Romans 12:18

[18] If it's possible—as far as it depends on you—be at peace with everyone.

Injil, Acts of the Apostles 10:34, 35

[34] Peter then said, "Now I know that God truly does not show favoritism

[35] But welcomes those among every nation who fear him and do what is right."

Terminology

God or Allah?

- Some associate the word "Allah" with the goddess al-Lāt who was worshipped in Petra (modern-day Jordan) in the pre-Islamic era.
- However, the Honored Quran vehemently distances itself from this assumption (see Al-Najm 53:19-23,27-28).
- Not only Muslims but also oriental Christians (Arabs, Arameans, and Maltese) and Arabic-speaking Jews have consistently named God "Allah" long before quranic Islam (end of the seventh century AD) and still do it today.
- That is why I keep the name Allah throughout the book in connection with Islam and the Honored Quran (otherwise, I call Him "God").

The Honored Bible

"Bible" stems from the Greek *biblos* (book). It consists of:

- The Old Testament, which largely corresponds to the *TaNaKh/Ta-nakh* of the Jews (*Tôrâh*, Arabic *Taurat*: also known as the Five Books of Moses/Musa $^{(Pbuh)}$); *Nəḇî'îm*: "Prophets"; and *Kətuḇîm*: "Scriptures." Hence, the abbreviation *TaNaKh*).
- The New Testament, which refers to the speeches, deeds, and life of Jesus $^{(piuh)}$ and his disciples.
- Muslims generally refer to the Honored Bible as "Taurat, Zabur, and Injil" (the Law, the Psalms, and the Gospels).
- Most readers may not be aware that, when mentioning divine revelations, the Honored Quran mainly uses "Allah's Word" (*kalim*^{u} and *kalimat*^{u}) for the Old Testament.

Muslim Terms of Respect

- Muslims only mention the Quran with respectful words like *sharīf* (honored) or *karīm* (precious). I chose "Honored" and use it for the Quran and the Bible.
- According to the Islamic habit, I placed the abbreviation "pbuh" after the names of the prophets as a *tasliya* (sign of respect) to be translated as "Peace be upon him." The plural is "pbut" ("Peace be upon them"). After Jesus (piuh), I use what Muslims use: "piuh" ("Peace is upon him").

Jesus (piuh)

Depending on the context, Jesus is referred to by his Christian name, Jesus, or by the Muslim equivalent: either Al-Masih Isa ibn Maryam (Al-Masīḥ 'Īsā Ibn Maryam) or simply Al-Masih.

Mary

Christians usually know the mother of Jesus (piuh) as "Mary." The original text of the New Testament, however, sometimes uses *María* (Greek) and sometimes *Maryám* (Aramaic). The original Hebrew form is Miriam. This is why I chose to call her Maryam.

Simplified Arabic Names

Prophets (pbut) common to Christianity and Islam are referred to by either their Christian or Muslim name depending on the context. To help both Muslim and non-Muslim readers, I have romanized the Arabic spelling of names as follows:

Adam (Ādam)	Adam
Allah (Allāh)	God (see explanation above)
Al-Masih Isa Ibn Maryam (Al-Masīḥ 'Īsā Ibn Maryam)	Jesus Christ, Son of Mary
Dawud (Dāūd)	David
Eva (Hawwa)	Eve
Ibrahim ('Ibrahīm)	Abraham

Harun (Hārūn)	Aaron
Ilyas (‘Ilyās)	Elijah
Ishaq (‘Isḥāq)	Isaac
Ishmael (‘Ismā‘īl)	Ishmael
Lut (Lūṭ)	Lot
Muhammad (Muḥammad)	Mohammed
Musa (Mūsā)	Moses
Nuh (Nūḥ)	Noah
Sulaiman (Sulaymān)	Solomon
Yahya (Yaḥyā)	John the Baptist
Yunus (Yūnus)	Jonah
Yusuf (Yūsuf)	Joseph
Yaqub (Ya’qūb)	Jacob
Zakariya (Zakariyyā)	Zachariah

The first time these names appear in the book, I will indicate both spellings (e.g., Abraham/Ibrahim).

Other Arabic Words

Ayah (*āyah*)	Chapter of the Quran, pl. ayat *(āyāt)*
Injil (*Injīl*)	The New Testament
Quran (*Qur’ān*)	The Koran
Shaytan (*Shaytān*)	Satan
Surah (*sūrah*)	quranic verse, pl. surat (*suwar*)
Hadith (*ḥadīth*)	Islamic tradition, pl. Hadiths (*aḥādīth*)
Tafsir (tafsīr)	Quranic exegesis
Taurat (Tawrāt)	The Torah (the Old Testament)
Zabur (Zabūr)	The Psalms

بسم الله الرحمن الرحيم

Chapter 1

The Quranic View on Christian Apostasy

Muslims are well aware that many Christians disregard the teachings of their Scriptures (Taurat, Zabur, and Injil). In that regard, the Honored Quran abounds in reproach against the "People of the Book." Some examples:

Al-Baqarah 2:75

> 75 Do you expect them to trust you when some of them listened to Allah's Word and corrupted it after having understood it?

Then, in the same surah, we read (Al-Baqarah, Ayah 170):

> 170 When they were told to follow what Allah had sent down, they said, "No, we follow what we found among our forefathers"—even though their fathers did not use reason and were not rightly guided.

The observation is echoed in 'Āli 'Imrān 3:78:

> 78 A fraction of them roll their tongues when they recite the Book. They want you to believe that this belongs to the Book while it does not, and they say it comes from Allah while it does not. In doing so, they lie—and they know it.

The quranic context essentially associates the "People of the Book" with the Jews, although similar rebukes were directed against those who call themselves *naṣārā,* "Christians":

Al-Mā'idah 5:14

[14] We made a covenant with those who call themselves Christians, but they forgot a part of what they were supposed to remember from it. We aroused enmity and hatred between them until the Resurrection Day. Soon, Allah will show them what they have done.

The Odyssey of Christianity

Before I explore the Honored Quran further, I will expose the process that produced what may be termed "apostasy" within Christianity. For this, it will be beneficial to briefly review the socioreligious context of the Middle Ages along with its negative culmination, often labeled the "Dark Ages."

Very soon after Jesus (piuh) was raised to Heaven, his followers suffered strong opposition.

On February 23, 303 AD, the Roman Emperor Diocletian ordered the newly built church in Nicomedia to be razed. This marked the beginning of the most serious waves of persecution early Christianity faced. By decree, places of worship were destroyed, properties confiscated, copies of the Honored Bible burnt, and Christians prevented from living their faith openly.

Yet even after the Roman authorities' repressive policies against those who refused to worship the emperor, things seemed to begin to look up for Christians. Galerius, Diocletian's adoptive son and follower, had been a strong enemy of Christianity. Eventually, he realized that all violent measures against Christians would remain inefficient.

That is why he finally changed his attitude and promulgated the Edict of Serdica in April 311, which gave Christians and non-Christians "the free choice to follow any religion, so that everything that contains divinity in the heavenly spheres may be appeased and favorable to us and those under our authority" (Lanarès 1975, pp. 6, 7). This change marked the official end of Roman ill-treatment and the victory of the new religion. All Christian prisoners were released and could henceforth practice their conviction without hindrance.

Another decisive move came two years later. Constantine, who had raised himself to the rank of *Imperator Maximus* while Galerius was still senior emperor, legalized the Christian faith across his empire. Even though it was one official religion among many, Constantine sided with Christianity. Very soon, the believers in Jesus (piuh) were granted complete protection and the right to worship unhindered according to their conscience. The Edict of Milan thus formally ended discrimination and granted Christianity the status of a fully-legal religion.

However, this positive turn in religious history eventually damaged Christianity more than it helped, and I need to spend some time trying to explain why.

"This positive turn in religious history eventually damaged Christianity more than it helped."

There has been much debate about the emperor's motivation for embracing Christianity. Was his choice motivated by political opportunism, or did a deep, heartfelt conviction drive him? The fact is that, parallel to the new religious liberty, non-Christian symbols slowly replaced Christian signs. For instance, in the basement of St. Peter's Basilica, one can still see a mosaic from Constantine's time on which Jesus (piuh) is portrayed as the sun god Apollo.

Constantine the Great continued to worship the "Unconquered Sun," a very popular god in the Roman Empire. He kept on issuing coins with the words *Sol Invictus* engraved on them. On March 7, 321 AD, he decreed that Sunday (*Dies Solis*) should be the Roman day of rest; i.e., a day off in honor of the late Roman deity *Sol Invictus.* This is the true historic reason why many Christians keep Sunday as a holiday, even though the Honored Bible specifies the seventh-day Sabbath as Allah's holy day of rest (Saturday, still called *sabt* in Arabic today).

In 330, Constantine transferred his throne from Rome to Byzántion, a tiny Greek colony named after King Býzas. The settlement became Néa Rhōmē (New Rome), but was soon changed into Constantinoúpolis (the city of Constantine; today's Istanbul). This was happening far from Rome, giving the Roman bishops the freedom to expand their power without much control. While the Roman Emperor focused on the empire's eastern part, the West was in a vacuum that allowed the official Christian religion to act on behalf of the government. In response, Constantine was ready to provide further recognition—which means more authority—to the head of the church in Rome. This would secure for him support from the religious authorities.

Yet in taking such a course, Constantine underestimated the potential of ancient Rome in the West. Just consider the vast distance between the new and the old Rome. He opened the door to self-determination that would be challenging to shut. From then on, the power of the Roman Church led her to several cases of abuse in the name of religion.

Pagan Elements

Many among the followers of Jesus (piuh) started to dilute the message of the Honored Bible, adding several pagan teachings. This is how it happened:

Constantine's friendly attitude toward Christianity resulted in the nominal conversion of millions of heathens to the "state church" throughout the Roman Empire. The suddenness of the switch implies that most of the new converts did not know what the message of Jesus (piuh) was about. Also at that time, people were mostly illiterate and had no access to the Honored Bible, so it was just as difficult to communicate the Truth to them as it was easy to "sell" them any misconception. Furthermore, the clergy were the only safeguard against political despots. The peasants often had poor intellectual and theological education, so their religious superiors were likely to abuse the trust put in them (after all, the naiveté and lack of knowledge of commoners have always made them easy prey for religious deceivers; we should never forget that humans believe too quickly).

Soon after the more-or-less forced baptism of hundreds of thousands of pagans, in a context where Christianity had reached the cities but not so much the outlands, pagan habits came back into daily life. The continuous arrival of non-Christianized barbarians reinforced the process.

So, the mix of ignorance and blind obedience opened the door to pagan elements. In addition, the teachings of philosophers received attention and played an important part in theological debates:

> Now the work of corruption rapidly progressed. Paganism, while appearing to be vanquished, became the conqueror. Her spirit controlled the Church. Her doctrines, ceremonies, and superstitions were incorporated into the faith and worship of the professed followers of Christ. (White 1911, p. 49.2)

While considering themselves "Christians," the Western populations kept some of their pagan traditions and mixed them with the newly-embraced religion. One superstition was added to another: magic formulas, trust in the supernatural power of relics, and pagan liturgies were widely introduced. For example, local heroes everywhere were declared holy and worshiped as "saints." And in southern Germany, many early Catholic places of worship were built on water sources—the very spots where pagans used to come and idolize the water coming from the earth as having magical power.

The Rise of the West Roman Church

The year 527 AD marks the beginning of Justinian I's reign. This Eastern Roman emperor was concerned about the intrusion of Germanic tribes into his realm. Fortunately, many newcomers converted to Catholicism and, by doing so, surrendered to the ecclesiastical authorities. At the same time, Justinian wanted to benefit from the Church's well-functioning administrative structure.

These reasons partly explain why Justinian tried to get the bishop of Rome on his side. In a letter addressed to Pope John II in 533, he urged the Orthodox patriarchs to accept the supremacy of the West Roman Church. However, if his purpose was to strengthen his authority, then instead he eventually reinforced the papacy's power and slowly transferred his imperial supremacy to the established Church. In the foreword of a letter sent to Pope John II's successor in 536, Justinian accepted the bishop of Rome's sovereignty, even trusting in his quasi-infallibility. This step is generally considered the beginning of the so-called "Dark Ages" in Europe. Lasting until the aftermath of the French Revolution, this period is described as "a long night of almost universal darkness, ignorance and superstition, with scarcely a ray of light to illuminate the gloom" (Dowling 1846, p. 181).

The dominant church reacted to Justinian by expressing her will to help maintain stability and imperial power. These are arts in which the clergy proved more reliable than many generals and governors. In their thirst for influence and to secure obedience, the pontifical authorities appointed civil servants eager to climb the administrative ladder. To achieve their goals, they did not hesitate to blend credulity with a good portion of spiritual abuse and season it generously with feigned godliness. Since religion has always appeared to be an adequate way to manipulate credulous minds, the recipe succeeded. Costly pilgrimages and acts of penance, the construction of imposing cathedrals, the veneration of relics, and the payment of large sums to the priests; these and many similar occupations were enjoined to appease God's wrath or gain His favor.

While during Constantine's governance politics had the last word over religious matters, the situation under Justinian was now reversed. Religion took over politics. The more power the religious authorities received, the more darkness fell upon the West.

Theological Implications

Before continuing, I wish to stress that this exposition of the facts is not intended to stigmatize any religion or any fervent follower of any faith. On the contrary, I would like to help any sincere person in his or her search for the Truth. This is not about individuals but about a system that led the Occident into an era of deep intellectual darkness, commonly called "the period of obscurantism."

As soon as the Church was guided by a mainly political agenda, she ceased to be moved by love for the Truth. Under such circumstances, mainline Christianity swiftly lost her destiny as the locus of biblical faith. The subsequent centuries witnessed a constant increase of errors within doctrinal precepts:

> The darkness seemed to grow more dense. Image worship became more general. Candles were burned before images, and prayers were offered to them. The most absurd and superstitious customs prevailed. The minds of men were so completely controlled by superstition that reason itself seemed to have lost its sway. While priests and bishops were themselves pleasure-loving, sensual, and corrupt, it could only be expected that the people who looked to them for guidance would be sunken in ignorance and vice. (White 1911, p. 57.1)

Titles like "God on earth" and "Our Lord God the Pope" further show the usurpation of power that happened then. But another forgery was needed to enable the Roman institutions to benefit from the fears and vices of her adherents. This was a stratagem called "purgatory," a kind of heavenly torture chamber in which the souls not wicked enough to deserve everlasting damnation were to undergo a mere "cleansing punishment" for their sins. Century after century, sincere believers were terrorized by the prospect of spending eternity in the fire. Then they were advised that, through monetary payments, they could try to free themselves from transgressions and even release the souls of their deceased friends and relatives from those tormenting flames. Eloquent portrayals from the curia's pulpits coerced people to accept in good faith anything that would supposedly spare them these ultimate agonies and open the way to Heaven once they had been relieved from impurity.

Since absolution was to be exclusively granted by the clergy, the forgery of purgatory enabled the Roman Church to benefit from the vices of her adherents.

Even worse were the extortions committed by priests who enriched their order at the expense of sincere humans. They insinuated that generous donations (even giving children to the Church) could alleviate the pain.

Later, complete remission of guilt past, present, and future was assured to whoever would enlist in the Crusades. Thus, the pontiffs hoped to enlarge their temporal dominion. At the same time, they claimed the right to exterminate those who dared to oppose their spiritual supremacy: "By such means did Rome fill her coffers and sustain the magnificence, luxury, and vice of the pretended representatives of Him who had not where to lay His head" (White 1911, 59.1).

To understand how such abuse could happen, we must bear in mind that, at that time, the clergy could easily justify any excess by claiming divine authority. Not too many had access to sufficient information to expose such a scam. Books were handwritten, so only the wealthiest could afford them. A publication like the Honored Bible would have cost as much as an entire flock of sheep. Illiteracy was high, and even the few literates scarcely comprehended the text since it was written in Latin.

That explains why, when the University of Paris published the first French edition of the sacred text (1226 to 1250), its success was overwhelming. It is also why it is no wonder that the Catholic Church immediately took action. For those able to read, Rome claimed that it was her office to interpret the Honored Bible, and issued an explicit interdiction to read it. In 1229, the Council of Toulouse stipulated:

> We forbid laypeople to own the Old and New Testament, except the Psalms, prayer books, and the Veneration of the Holy Virgin Mary. We categorically forbid these books to be owned in a translated edition into any common language. (Mansi 1779)

Only five years later, in 1234, the Synod of Tarragona amended:

> No one has the right to own the Old and New Testament in Romanic language. Whoever owns them should hand them to the nearest bishop to be burnt. If not, whether he is a clergyman or a layman, he will be suspected of heresy until he is cleared of every doubt. (Mirbt 1924, p. 194)

At the same time, the ecclesiastic traditions rose to enjoy the level of quasi-divine inspiration. As early as 787, the Second Council of Nicaea had declared, "Whoever rejects the Church tradition—written and oral—must be excommunicated" (Uhlmann 1984, p. 12). The power of the clergy over illiterate people is how spiritual abuse seems to have been almost unlimited.

Apostasy Today?

Christians have filled history with sad records of beliefs and acts that do not speak for the authenticity of their faith, either because their authentically-held faith was improperly exercised or because they were not truly following that faith. However, we should be aware that these beliefs and acts have nothing in common with the beautiful message of the Honored Bible. Even so, someone may say that since then, western countries have left behind the obscurantism of the Dark Ages. This is why I wonder to what extent deviation from the Honored Bible still affects Christianity today.

- *The Crusades*: Who has not heard of this unequaled source of suffering for the Islamic population in the Near East (conducted in the name of religion)? These shameful actions of savagery and inhumanity—the massacres, pogroms, deportations, looting, devastating breaking of confidence, and infidelity—were not just directed against Islam. The Crusades harmed millions of Jews and Christians as well.
- *Colonial wars and crimes*: How many acts of fanaticism and intolerance, up to the trade of whole African tribes to America for slavery, have been conducted in the name of Allah?
- *The theory of evolution*: It has been widely accepted among Christians as a fact, so that many no longer believe that Allah created the world with His mighty hand and great wisdom.
- *The authority of the Honored Bible*: Christians speak about the Honored Bible in an irreverent way, undermining divine inspiration.
- *Spirituality*: Religion has been gradually removed from social life. Most Christians do not even dare to pray in public anymore.
- *Destructive habits*: Especially in countries with a Christian cultural background, human beings, Allah's highest creatures on earth, defile themselves. They destroy themselves with alcohol, tobacco, drugs, pornography, and other vices.

Al-kāfirūn (The Concealers)

Therefore, it is quite understandable that many believers reject *that* kind of Christianity and see it as *kufr bi-Allah* (blasphemy). For instance,

Muhammad Anwar es-Sadat, who was awarded the Nobel Peace Prize for his efforts towards reconciliation, once said:

> The West offends against truth, history, and human values. Does it have the right to interpret the Christian message in a way that contradicts the fundamental principles of Christianity? By no means will we in the East accept that.
>
> [...]
>
> Since Christianity has its roots in the Orient, we Orientals know it is based on the two fundamental principles of faith and love. Can we find these two in what the West calls 'Christianity'? (Berthier 1985, p. 151)

Only *Some* of Them

Indeed, the Honored Quran is correct in rebuking the People of the Book for not following the teachings of the Honored Bible. Such "concealers" have covered up (*kafara*) the godly message and neglected it in favor of their traditions.

However, we must be careful not to commit a fatal mistake. The Honored Quran does not expressly state that Christians have falsified the text. It becomes clear when you reread the ayah quoted at the beginning of this chapter, Al-Baqarah 2:75:

> 75 Do you expect them to trust you when some of them listened to Allah's Word and corrupted it after having understood it?

Note that the reproach only concerns "some of them"; i.e., *one specific group* among the People of the Book. A corruption of the text on the part of such a group would mean that there are currently two different Bibles in circulation: the genuine version and a falsified one. Yet this is not the case. Conversely, there must be a majority of Jews and Christians (more than "some") who have put into practice biblical instructions without mixing them with human hermeneutics.

Further, the affirmation that "they have perverted it knowingly after they had understood it" implies that they first listened to the actual text, i.e., they still had it. Consequently, those who did not pervert the text must also still have the accurate text in their hands. Let us look at a second ayah:

Al-Baqarah 2:170

170 When they were told to follow what Allah had sent down, they said, "No, we follow what we found among our forefathers"—even though their fathers did not use reason and were not rightly guided.

The negative answer to the admonition to "follow what Allah had sent down" implies that the distortion merely consists of the refusal to listen to what God has revealed. As I will develop in the next chapter, it does not mean that the text *per se* was corrupted. Interestingly, these ayat name the Honored Bible "Allah's Word" or "what Allah has sent down."

I encourage all of us to turn away from the falsehoods taught by certain alleged disciples of Jesus (piuh) and, at the same time, to discover and follow the Truth. But how can we identify what is right and what is wrong? The answer is simple: read the Honored Bible!

If you carefully read the Honored Taurat, Zabur, and Injil, you will discover what they teach and what they don't. In earlier times, Christians had little access to the Honored Bible and might be excused for their ignorance. Nowadays, however, almost anyone who looks for the text can find access to it. Published as "The Holy Bible," it is printed in over 3,000 languages, and anyone can download it online. Therefore, I wonder why some among the followers of Jesus (piuh) ignore such clear commands.

The answer is that human-made traditions and convenience tend to be stronger than the Truth. Many do not read the Honored Bible or interpret them as if they were no longer binding. If this is so, the issue is not whether or not the text of the Honored Bible has been changed, but that some professed Christians do not study it—or interpret the text according to their wishes. This is the only explanation for why ungodly conduct like racism and wars could arise again and again in history, even sometimes in the name of Allah. However, Jesus (piuh) has declared:

Injil, Gospel of Matthew 22:39

39 Love your neighbor as yourself.

To clarify, let me illustrate: Even if good soap is available in every supermarket, some people are dirty. Should someone blame the soap for it? Of course not! The responsibility lies with those who do not use it!

They Are Not All Alike

Another consideration is that the accusation is not directed against *all* the People of the Book but only against *some*. A closer look at the text shows that it is addressed to the Jews and not to the Christians. Even if you want to include these latter, this quranic statement implies that not *all* People of the Book are *kuffār*.[2] On the contrary, one group of Christians follows the instructions of the Honored Bible correctly, without mixing them with human traditions or interpretations.

At the same time, several ayat reveal deep sympathy for the authentic followers of Jesus (piuh). A statement found in Surah 'Āli 'Imrān should particularly draw our attention, in which Ayah 104 expresses the wish that there should be "a community … that calls for the good, enjoins the proper, and forbids wrongdoing." These are "those [who] will succeed":

> Several ayat reveal deep sympathy for the authentic followers of Jesus (piuh).

'Āli 'Imrān 3:104

> 104 Let a community come forth from you that calls for the good, enjoins the proper, and forbids wrongdoing. Those (believers) will succeed.

The community originated "from you," which indicates that it includes those who accepted the message of Muhammad (pbuh). But the next ayah, 105, warns Muslims not to be "like those who are divided":

> 105 And do not be like those who are divided. They have turned away from the clear evidence that came to them. They will obtain severe punishment.

The ayah does not specify which persons are involved. One of the next ayat, 110, establishes a distinction among the People of the Book, accompanied by the wish that "they may believe":

> 110 You are the best community that has ever arisen for humanity. You command what is right, forbid wrongdoing, and believe in Allah. It would have been suitable for the People of the Book to believe. Some of them do, but most of them are insolent.

Let us note that, even if "most of them" are insolent, "some (among them) believe," and that is where Ayat 113 and 114 take up the thread of the idea by specifying:

2 Generally translated as "unbeliever," *kuffār* stems from *kafara* (to cover) and means "those who cover [the truth]."

'Āli 'Imrān 3:113, 114

> 113 They are not all alike. Among the People of the Book, a community stands for the right [or a righteous community]. They dwell on Allah's verses during the night hours in an attitude of adoration.
> 114 They believe in Allah and the Day After, enjoin what is right, forbid what is wrong, and hasten in good works. They are among the righteous.

But is it legitimate to apply the expression "those who are among the righteous" to Jews and possibly Christians? If so, Christians would be put on an equal level with Muslims as far as faith is concerned.

Muslim scholarship mainly chooses to limit the application of this ayah to some Christians and Jews who, at the time of Muhammad (pbuh), converted to Islam, such as Abū-Salama, one of the early companions of the Messenger. Others apply them to the Christians who agreed with *tawḥīd* (the oneness of Allah). There is no real consensus in Islam about the Christian identity of these "among the righteous" introduced in 'Āli 'Imrān 3:113, 114. However, the ambiguity disappears if we put Ayat 110, 113, and 114 side by side:

- The statement "some of the People of the Book do not believe" is generally applied to Christians, but Ayat 113 and 114 distinguish them from Christians "who are not alike."
- Like Muslims, "they (those who are not alike) enjoin what is right and forbid what is wrong" (the exact Arabic wording in 3:110 and 114).
- Both groups (Muslims and apostolic Christians) believe in Allah and the Day After.
- Therefore, the followers of Jesus (piuh) are "believers"—just like the followers of Muhammad (pbuh).
- Both are part of one united body (the same word, *'umma*, applied to both).
- There is no indication that they embraced a new religion called Islam or recited the *Shahāda* (confession of faith).
- The expression "they (these Christians) are among the righteous" (*min l-ṣāliḥīna*) implies that Muslims should accept those peculiar Christians as being equally worthy candidates for Paradise (*ṣāliḥ*: suitable for Paradise).

If my perception is correct, I may expect more ayat reflecting the same categorization. The text supporting my assumption is Al-Mā'idah 5:82:

> [82] For sure, you will find the enemies of the believers among the Jews and those who associate, and you will find the nearest to the believers among those who say, "We are Christians." Indeed, among them are men who are devoted to learning, have renounced the world, and are not arrogant.

The statement "Among them are men who are devoted to learning, have renounced the world (literally: priests and monks) and are not arrogant" implies that not all Christians are like these and that there are two groups of followers of Jesus (piuh). What is essential is that some Christians, no matter what percentage of them, are different from the majority and that Muslims should identify them as "nearest to them."

The Honored Quran emphasizes a contrast between "the Jews, the adoptionist" (those who *ashrakū*: associate; the same word as *mush'rikūn*) on one side and the *naṣārā*, "Christians," on the other. That the latter is "nearest in love to the believers" can be understood as advice not to brand all Christians "unbelievers" or enemies but to look for friendship with "the nearest."

The question is whether the distinction made between two Christian groups still applies today. Where are those who are humble, pious, and ready to be "the nearest to the Muslims"? The fact is that history has taken this into account.

Muhammad (pbuh) and His Followers' Attention to Christianity

History records that Muhammad (pbuh) himself, at the very beginning of quranic Islam, praised unwavering Christians as fully submitted (*muslimūn*) to Allah in the same way he was. He who preached the one and only God and fought against the pagan deities showed consideration for them:

- In 615 AD, he advised some Muslims to flee the polytheists' oppression in Makka and look for asylum in the (Christian) kingdom of Ethiopia.
- In 630 AD, he invited the Christians from Aba as-Sa'ud to celebrate Easter in the Mosque of Medina.
- He spread out his cloak to enable Christian guests to sit on it.
- Whenever Christians were oppressed for any reason, he would grant them refuge.

It is said that, as soon as Abū Bakr, the first caliph, established his authority, he sent a message to his army leader Usāma ibn Zayid:

> "Remember that you are always in Allah's presence, on the verge of death, assured of judgment, and hopeful of Paradise. Avoid injustice and oppression, consult with your brethren, and study to preserve the love and confidence of your troops.
>
> […]
>
> "Let not your victory be stained with the blood of women and children. Destroy no palm trees nor burn any fields of corn. Cut down no fruit trees, nor do any mischiefs to cattle, only such as you kill to eat. When you make any covenant or article, stand to it and be as good as your word.
>
> […]
>
> "As you go on, you will find some religious persons who live retired in monasteries and propose to themselves to serve God that way: let them in peace and neither kill them nor burn their monasteries." (quoted in Gibbon 2006, p. 189f)

Unfortunately, the historical records do not specify the identity of these Christians. We only know they were "religious persons who lived retired in monasteries." While they were hated and excommunicated by the dominant religion, Muslims in Egypt protected them. Similar cases were witnessed during the Islamic expansion in different places (cf. Aṭ-Ṭabarī 1968, p. 246).

But how can you identify the genuine followers of Jesus (piuh)? Where can you find them these days?

From the earliest centuries, Christianity was divided between the dominant state religion and those who tried to remain devoted to the message of Jesus (piuh) in its purity. The foundational beliefs of these faithful Christians were:

- The study of the Honored Bible as the only divine source of revelation.
- Belief in the salvation of humanity thanks to God's mercy and not acquired by means of money or other good deeds.
- The validity of the Ten Commandments as revealed in God's Word (Exodus 20:1-17) and as Jesus (piuh) interpreted them (The Gospel of Matthew, Chapters 5-7).
- Rejection of the union between religious and political authorities.

As we have already read in Al-Mā'idah 5:82, the Honored Quran praises "the nearest to the believers among those who say, 'We are Christians!'" The statement insists on their humility: "Indeed, among them are men (who are) devoted to learning, have renounced the world, and are not arrogant." Indeed, it is just as essential to live a religion humbly and respectfully as it is to put forward dogmas, no matter how accurate they may be.

Christians Persecuted by "Christians"

Needless to say, Bible-oriented Christians have been systematically oppressed by the state Church throughout the centuries:

> It was the policy of Rome to obliterate every trace of dissent from her doctrines or decrees. Everything heretical, whether persons or writings, she sought to destroy. Expressions of doubt, or questions as to the authority of papal dogmas, were enough to forfeit the life of rich or poor, high or low. (White 1911, 61.2)

Institutional Christianity began to fight against so-called "heretics." The following quotation gives us an idea of the atrocities committed against the authentic followers of Jesus (piuh):

> Over five centuries, from the establishment of the Inquisition by Pope Innocent IV in 1252 to the time of the Enlightenment, the guardians of the faithful believers in Christ have drawn a gruesome trail of blood. According to widely diverging estimates, between one and ten million people have been driven to death by life, most of them burned alive. (Wensierski et al. 1998, p. 32)

Add to this figure thousands of Jews between the eleventh and fourteenth century (Mynarek 1999, p. 187), sixty thousand supposed witches (Tremp 2014), and millions of victims of the conquest of South America. Some writers go far beyond:

> Credible historians have estimated that more than fifty million of the human family have been slaughtered for 'the crime' of heresy by popish persecutors, an average of more than forty thousand religious murders for every year of the existence of Popery.[3] (Dowling 1846, p. 181)

3 John Dowling adds: "However, no computation can reach the number who have been put to death on account of their maintaining the profession of the Gospel and opposing the corruption of the Church of Rome. One million Waldenses perished in France, and nine hundred thousand Orthodox Christians

Christians Protected by Muslims

At the same time, whenever Christians were discriminated against, Muslims gladly provided refuge to them. Even in the time of the Arabic conquests[4], "while Muslims couldn't trade and reside in most Christian lands, Christians could live in many Islamic societies as 'People of the Book'" (Goffman 2002, p. 15).[5] Whenever people were ill-treated for their faith (Treadgold 1997, p. 350), the Islamic-ruled countries gladly granted protection to those who chose to remain loyal to their convictions and refused to compromise.

> "Islamic-ruled countries gladly granted protection to those who remained loyal to their convictions."

The same happened with the Nestorian Christians[6] around 910 AD. Muslims offered these Christians a haven of peace. At that time the metropolis of Baghdad welcomed between 40,000 and 50,000 of them (Kirk 2006, p. 22). Also:

> The Eastern Christian Church, which had been persecuted and excommunicated by the Western Church, was not destroyed by Islam. The first physicians in the Muslim centers of medical learning and treatment were Nestorian medical professionals. (Phillips 2003, p. 4)

Such Christian refugees were welcomed, as respected Islamic scholars write:

> When the Arab Christians were hereticated (sic) by the Church of Rome and persecuted by the Byzantine Empire, they took refuge in the desert.
>
> [...]

---

were slain in less than thirty years after the institution of the order of the Jesuits. The Inquisition destroyed, by various tortures, one hundred and fifty thousand within thirty years ...."

4 Arab conquests did not happen without blood being spilled on both sides, and the quranic texts speaking of "killing infidels" have often been overinterpreted. However, the term "infidel" (*mushriq*, thirty-seven times in the Honored Quran) does not apply to Christians in general but to those who preached Adoptionism (cf. Chapter 3 of this book; see also Al-Īsra' 17:111 and Al-Fur'qān 25:2). Likewise, texts such as At-Tawbah 9:5 should be read in their precise context ("When the holy months are over")—similarly, Al-Mā'idah 5:33, according to which self-defense is encouraged in case of attack and deterrence.

5 For example, in 722 AD, the Byzantine Emperor Leo III forced all Jews and dissenters to be baptized; and Leo V (813-820 AD) executed the Paulicians, who lived according to the Honored Bible.

6 A specific group of Christians.

> Both Jews and Christian immigrants to the desert found a ready welcome among those Arabs who upheld the Mesopotamian-Abrahamic tradition. Together, they consolidated that tradition in Peninsular Arabia. (al Faruqi and al Faruqi 1986, p. 61)

Henry Treece, renowned for his research on the Crusades, summarizes the religious freedom under Arab governance in the following terms:

> Under the liberal and tolerant Moslem regime, most Christians of the lost Eastern Empire became indifferent to the claims of the weakened Emperor of Constantinople.
>
> […]
>
> The Christians in the East paid their poll tax to the Saracens, at a lower rate than their own Emperor had once exacted, and went on with their almost uninterrupted worship, delighted at the lack of persecution. As for the heretics among the Christians, their hearts rejoiced at the domination of the Arabs—may God strengthen it and prosper it.
>
> […]
>
> The fact was that the Arabs, unlike the Eastern Emperors, were realists. They accepted a tax in lieu of military service, guaranteed the rights of belief of all whose religion was based on the Bible, and allowed each sect to live as a self-governing community within the Arab state. Christians were even allowed to build new churches, provided they did not overtop the mosques in height! (Treece 1962, p. 157)

The Ottoman Empire

The Ottoman Empire deserves special recognition for its unique tolerance. The historian Leften Stavrianos brings out the Ottoman openness in contrast with the bigotry of the Christian West. To quote the Greek historian:

> The Ottoman Empire was unique […] for its unequaled degree of religious tolerance. In a period when Catholics and Protestants were massacring each other and when Jews were being hounded from one Christian state to another, the subjects of the sultan were free to worship as they wished with comparatively minor disabilities. (Stavrianos 2008, p. 232)

Daniel Goffman adds:

> The Ottomans drew upon the egalitarianism and inclusive traditions of Central Asia and the relative tolerance of Islam to construct a society in which non-Muslim monotheists could live and work in relative freedom. Oppressed inhabitants of exclusionary Christian states found such an alternative enormously attractive. (Goffman 2002, p. 47)

It would be naïve to make out as if there have never been any problems or conflicts between Muslims and Christians. Not all of them were as open-minded as the Ottomans in their best years.[7]

Nevertheless, even if with time such a good neighborhood was lost in many cases, I want to accentuate the overall positive relationship between the two religions. Human history is filled with injustices committed in the name of religion, and crimes have been perpetrated on both sides. If so, the time has come to confess and avoid the past's faults by moving forward in a spirit of humility and respect. In that regard, I invite you to reread the introduction of this book that laid the groundwork for our study: burying the hatchet and building bridges.

Back to the Roots of Islam

From the perspective of a cordial understanding between Christians and Muslims, have you maybe wondered how it comes to be that Muslims have been so kind to these genuine Christians?

Part of the answer might be that the root of the word *islām,* as the principle of submission[8], does not refer to any specific religious group.

I conclude that all faithful followers of Jesus (piuh) must be considered *muslimūn*, "submitting" (to God).

7 You may perhaps wonder why Muslims were so kind to these followers of Jesus (piuh). Some argue that tolerance was calculated goodness, first because of the *dhimmī* (a protective covering) against a *cizya* (poll tax) to be paid by non-Muslims. But by allowing conquered people to keep their religion, the conquerors preserved their identity and took away a primary reason to revolt; in other words, the less their subjects felt oppressed and disturbed in their rights and customs, the more they would be satisfied and accept new governance. The *dhimmī* might have motivated the Muslims to keep Christians as they were, i.e., as a source of extra income, while Christians could have seen this as a pragmatic ground to leave Christianity and join Islam. On the other hand, one non-negligible advantage of being a non-Muslim was exemption from serving in the military. In such a win-win situation, coexistence generally worked well. The old sociological rule might have applied in the long run: the less pressure, the better the result.

8 *Aslama*: to submit oneself. *Muslīm*: someone who submits (his will and entire life) to Allah; or, more precisely: the one standing under Allah's command.

Notice what the Honored Injil states on that matter:

Injil, Epistle of Paul to the Romans 12:1:

[1] By the mercy of God, I encourage you, brothers, to offer your bodies as a living sacrifice, holy and pleasing to God. This is your proper worship.

Here the Apostle Paul suggests that we should be subjected to Allah. Interestingly, the foundation of our "subjection to Allah" is His *raḥmāh* (compassion). It is the divine attribute occurring most often in the Honored Quran; in other words—using Muslim language—we may say that because Allah is the Merciful (Ar-Raḥmān) and the Compassionate (Ar-Raḥīm), we should be subjected (*aslama, taslim*) to Him. That is why the Apostle James exhorts his readers as follows:

Injil, Epistle of James 4:7, 8

7 Submit to God and resist the devil. And he will flee from you.
8 Draw near to God and he will draw near to you. Cleanse your hands, sinners, and purify your hearts, you hypocrites!

Needless to say, Paul's and James's concept of submission is in pure harmony with what the Honored Quran states:

Al-Baqarah 2:132

[132] And this is the legacy Ibrahim left to his sons, and Yaqub did the same: "Oh my sons! Allah has defined what you owe Him. Do not die except in the state of submission."

An-Nisā' 4:125

[125] Who is better in religion than he who fully submits to Allah while doing good and following the state of mind of Ibrahim, the upright in faith? Allah chose him as a friend.

Al-Ḥajj 22:78

[78] Strive[9] for Allah with the effort due to Him. He has chosen you and not laid upon you any hardship in religion. The state of mind of your father Ibrahim is yours. He named you Muslims long ago so that the Messenger may be your reference and you may testify to

9 The verb used here is *jāhada* (to be under tension); hence the figurative meaning: "to struggle." The use of the word *jihad* in the Honored Quran refers to a tension of a *spiritual* nature and not only *warlike*, as the text adds: "no religious constraint, except the way of your father Ibrahim who once called you submitted." All the other indications of *jāhada* (At-Tawbah 9:73, At-Taḥrīm 66:9, and Al-Ḥajj 22:78) are set in a spiritual context (faith, repentance, good deeds).

your fellow men. Therefore, attend your prayers, render your offerings, and hold fast to Allah, for He is your Guardian—a gracious Guardian and Helper!

According to these statements, all those who follow the example of Ibrahim (pbuh) *are Muslims* in the actual meaning of the term (submitting), and that explains why the Honored Quran considers all dedicated Christians to be "Muslims." Several ayat confirm that definition:

'Āli 'Imrān 3:52

52 And when Isa perceived some unbelief in them, he said: "Who shall be my helpers for Allah?" The apostles said: "We are Allah's helpers. We believe in Allah! Testify that we are submitting to Him (*mus'limūn*)!"

Al-Mā'idah 5:111

111 And when I inspired the Apostles to believe in Me and My messenger, they said: "We believe! Testify that we are submitting to Him (*mus'limūn*)!"

Taken in its original sense, the word *islām* means much more than a religious affiliation. It encompasses all those who consciously practice daily "submission" to Allah without primarily applying to any specific believers.

In the same way, the word *muslim* qualifies anyone "submitted" to Allah without appurtenance to a specific group or a religion. Indeed, we should consider faithful Christians as truly submitting (*muslimūn*) to Allah.

That is why the renowned scholar Syed Ameer Ali affirms, "There is no real difference between true Islam and true Christianity" (Ameer 2015, p. 179).

"No real difference between true Islam and true Christianity"—that sounds like a viable bridge to each other!

An Important Remark and a Cordial Invitation

Let me pause and make one remark.

I did not write this book to promote syncretism or push someone to deny his convictions. After all, the Truth is and remains the Truth. My sole intention is to share the biblical and quranic principle of submission to God as a shared value, as I believe that it is time to realize that both religions are much closer to each other than most believers on both sides may think.

The Honored Quran invites every believer to consider spending time with the Christians who live according to the Honored Bible:

Al-'Ankabūt 29:46

> 46 If you argue with the People of the Book, do it only in the most courteous way—except with those who do wrong; and say: "We believe in what has been sent down to you and us. Our God and your God is one, and we submit to Him."

At first glance, the "we" of the expression "we submit to Him" (*wa naḥnu lahu muslimūna*) could apply to Muslims in opposition to Christians ("you"). However, the previous expression "our God and your God is one" (*ilāhunā wa-ilāhukum wāḥidun*) insists on the fact that both religions have the same God (the One God). The quranic application of the word *muslim* to "those Jews and Christians who do not do wrong" confirms this interpretation.

Another ayah invites the reader to look for someone who knows the Honored Bible well in case of unanswered questions:

Yūnus 10:94

> 94 If you have any doubt concerning what We have sent down to you, ask those who read the Book before you. The Truth comes from your Lord. Therefore, do not be among those who doubt.

"Ask those who read the Book before you." This invitation explains why a growing number of Muslims have decided to break the wall. Many are trying to get acquainted with Bible-oriented Christians. They have understood what Christians *really* should be. They are searching the Sacred Scriptures to get to know the "People of the Book" better. I invite you to look for possibilities to dialogue with them.

- If you long for Allah's will,
- If you take the words of the Honored Quran seriously,
- Then look for those who have read the Honored Bible.
- Ask them everything you have kept asking for such a long time;
- Only argue with the faithful Christians "in the most courteous way,"
- And do not neglect "the Truth coming from your Lord."

Please do not hesitate to send us your comments! I value every opinion, and at the same time, it will be a pleasure to help you identify the authentic Christians described in the Honored Injil as "those who keep God's commands":

Injil, Revelation 14:12

> 12 This is the perseverance of God's people, of those who keep his commandments and remain attached to Jesus.

Moreover, if you read this book as a Christian, let me encourage you to come back to the pure teachings of the Honored Bible, to cherish and follow them, as it is said in the Honored Quran in 'Āli 'Imrān 3:71:

> 71 O People of the book, why do you mix the Truth with errors and hide the Truth while you know (what is right)?

Some Verses from the Honored Bible

Related to Chapter 1

The Concept of *Islām* in the Honored Bible

You may be surprised to hear that the word *islām* is biblical. Indeed, the Hebrew verb *šālām* occurs several times in the Honored Taurat. Its causative stem, *hišlîmū*, is the equivalent of the Arabic *yaslamu*. Mainly translated as "to make peace," it expresses the idea of subjection.

In addition to the text already quoted in this chapter (Romans 12:1), the principle of submission to God is fundamental in the Honored Bible and mentioned many times, for example, in the Honored Injil:

Injil, Epistle of James 4:7

7 Submit to God and resist the devil. And he will flee from you.

Apostasy Foretold

Injil, Gospel of Matthew 7:21

21 Not everyone who says to me (Jesus), "Lord, Lord!" will enter the Kingdom of Heaven, but only those who do the will of my Father in Heaven.

Injil, Gospel of Matthew 24:5, 24

5 Many will come in my name, claiming to be the Messiah, and will deceive many.

24 Indeed, false messiahs and false prophets will arise and show great signs and wonders to deceive even the chosen.

Injil, Acts of the Apostles 20:29, 30

29 I know that wild wolves will appear among you after I leave and that they will not spare the flock.

30 Men will rise among you and distort the truth to draw the disciples after them.

Injil, 2nd Epistle of Paul to the Thessalonians 2:3, 4

3 Let no one deceive you in any way, for that day will not come until the apostasy has begun and the man of lawlessness is revealed, the man doomed to destruction.

4 He will oppose and exalt himself over all that is called God and is worshiped, setting himself up in God's temple and claiming to be God himself.

Not all Christians are Apostates

Injil, Acts of the Apostles 18:9, 10

9 Don't be afraid! Speak up and don't be silent!

10 For I am with you, and no one will attack you or harm you, because I have many people in this city who follow my way.

Injil, Epistle of Paul to the Ephesians 5:8-11

8 Before you were darkness; now you are light in the Lord. Behave as children of light.

9 For the fruit of light is goodness, righteousness and truth.

10 Test what pleases the Lord,

11 And do not join in the vain works of darkness. On the contrary, you will discover them.

Injil, Epistle of Paul to the Philippians 2:15

15 Your life must be beyond criticism and transparent, as exemplary children of God in the midst of a corrupt, even perverted society, in which you must shine like stars in the night.

بسم الله الرحمن الرحيم

Chapter 2

The Honored Injil—A Corrupted Book?

Praise be to Allah, the Creator and Sustainer of the universe, the Owner of all things! He has given all human beings freedom of choice and shown them the Right Way often mentioned in the Honored Bible and the Honored Quran . I may compare His revelations to a road map guiding humanity toward eternal life. Talking about everlasting values, no one needs to get lost!

Have you ever gotten off track? If so, then you have felt that scary moment of disorientation. Driving in a big city with no idea how to reach your destination; being in the desert and the compass ceases to work; walking in an unknown area without a landmark; a child being lost in a bazaar or a mall. We all share the need for orientation, like a young adult facing several possibilities of education or the choice of whom to marry. So many decisions! In a very complicated world, we are like wanderers at night and need reliable advice and devices.

Fortunately, road maps, apps, and GPS make it easier to reach unknown destinations these days. What would happen, however, if the map were inaccurate? It may be an old edition. Or how would it be if someone falsified your GPS to mislead you? That would be rather time-consuming and quite unsafe.

Misleading someone on purpose is irresponsible. In business, circulating rumors can be considered a criminal offense. Some media outlets are sometimes accused of spreading fake news. The challenge is to identify whether there is a similar phenomenon in the religious field.

Indeed, some believers claim that Christians have altered the Honored Bible. It is a severe accusation and a cause of anger against the so-called "People of the Book." For good reason: Is there any greater sin than distorting Allah's Word?

Has the Honored Bible been corrupted? Is it conceivable that millions of Christians are mistaken? Of course, everything is thinkable, and if this accusation is the case, we need to be aware of the seriousness of the situation. Suppose millions of sincere believers have followed a distorted "road map" for nearly two thousand years; isn't it our solemn duty to help them? In the face of such a deception, we must do our best to lead them to the Truth.

As we ask Allah to accept our daily prayer of guidance into the Right Way (Al-Fātiḥah 1:6, 7), our most sincere wish should be that many Christians might also follow the Right Way. As it is written:

6 Guide us in the Right Way,

7 The path of those to whom you have consented, not those whose destiny is His wrath, nor those who go astray.

Let us go one step further: if the previous revelations have been altered, we must reject them. But if they have not been altered, we must eliminate our prejudices and withdraw our accusations. As you now realize, we need to study the matter very carefully.

“If the previous revelations have not been altered, we must eliminate our prejudices and withdraw our accusations.”

Why? No one will be ready to take us seriously if we do not have evidence to prove falsifications. Thus, concerning the well-known warning of the Honored Quran, finding an answer is of the highest importance:

An-Nisā' 4:136

136 O you who believe! Believe in Allah and His Messenger, in the Book He has sent down to His Messenger, and in the Book He has previously sent down. Whoever hides (something) about Allah, His angels, His Scriptures, His Messengers, and the Day After has lost his way and drifted away.

The text urges us to believe in *all* the books, which implies that the Sacred Scriptures in circulation at the time the Honored Quran was given must have been trustworthy. But how can we be sure that it is so?

The Testimony of the Honored Quran

Does the Honored Quran declare a potential falsification in the Honored Bible? There are numerous statements about it, and we must understand them correctly. In six surat, Jews—and possibly, but not explicitly, Christians—get a rebuke for not living according to their Sacred Scriptures:

- Al-Baqarah 2:41, 42, 58, 59, 78, 79, 140-143, 146, 159, 174
- ‘Āli ‘Imrān 3:71, 78, 187
- An-Nisā’ 4:46, 47
- Al-Mā’idah 5:13-15, 41
- Al-An‘ām 6:91
- Al-A‘rāf 7:162, 165

These are the texts generally quoted. In them the Arabic language uses eight different verbs. Here is a list of the first seven. Then I will look more closely at the most important one, which is *ḥarrafa* (to falsify).

- *akhfā* (to conceal, to hide): Al-Mā’idah 5:15; Al-An‘ām 6:91
- *baddala* (to replace words): Al-Baqarah 2:59; Al-A‘rāf 7:162
- *ishtarā* (to buy, to exchange; i.e., to make a cheap imitation): Al-Baqarah 2:79
- *katama* (to hide. The verb is used more frequently than the others): Al-Baqarah 2:42, 140, 146, 159, 174; ‘Āli ‘Imrān 3:71, 187
- *labas* (to clothe; i.e., to disguise the Truth [with lies]): Al-Baqarah 2:42; ‘Āli ‘Imrān 3:71
- *lawā lisān* (to roll the tongue): ‘Āli ‘Imrān 3:78; An-Nisā’ 4:46
- *nasiya* (to forget): Al-Mā’idah 5:13; Al-A‘rāf 7:165

Each one of these ayat gives details about what happened:

- Some Jews denied that Ibrahim and Muhammad (pbut) had the same faith.
- Some disagreed on the *qiblah* (direction in which to pray).
- Some did not read out the Honored Taurat correctly.
- Some sealed one particular scroll.
- Some put other books on the level of the Sacred Scriptures.

This list requires a few comments:

- The points of criticism concern only Jews. None of these reproaches is addressed directly to Christians. Therefore, none can apply to the New Testament.
- It concerns only *some* of the Jews. In this case, we should have two versions of the Old Testament, which is not the case.
- None of these verbs indicates a corruption of the Honored Taurat.

- Instead, some used incorrect pronunciation .
- Some of these ayat suggest an *oral* twisting, or the use of some words outside of their context.
- The fact that some used to partly forget the text after reading it does not imply that they took some portions away or that they changed the initial content.
- That is why, as previously mentioned, the Honored Taurat is still called "Allah's Word" (or "His Word").

The Meaning of *Ḥarrafa*

However, I must acknowledge four different ayat that I have not yet investigated, in which the verb *ḥarrafa* occurs:

- Al-Baqarah 2:75
- An-Nisā' 4:46
- Al-Mā'idah 5:13
- Al-Mā'idah 5:41

Let us have a closer look at these four ayat one by one! The first mention of *ḥarrafa* is found in Surah Al-Baqarah 2:75:

> 75 Do you expect them to trust you when some of them listened to Allah's Word and corrupted it after having understood it?

Here, the Honored Bible is called "Allah's Word,"[10] which speaks in favor of its validity and inspiration.

The second ayah in which the verb *ḥarrafa* occurs is Surah An-Nisā' 4:46:

> 46 Among the Jews there are some who displace the words from their right places and say: "We hear and we disobey," and "Listen, it would have been better not to hear," and "Observe," with a twist of their tongues and a disrespect to faith. If only they had said: "We hear and we obey," and "Hear," and "Look at us!" It would have been better for them, and more proper; but Allah has cursed them for their unbelief; and few of them will believe.

Like in the previous ayah, the *taḥrif* (twisting) refers to some "among the Jews." Christians are not implicated. Moreover, the sentence "They

10 [38] No Muslim would like to apply this text to the Honored Quran!

displace words from their right places" implies the intention to change the interpretation and *not* the text. That is why the "twisting" was oral ("of the tongue") and did not affect the content of the text.

The third instance of *ḥarrafa* is to be read in Surah Al-Mā'idah 5:13:

> 13 Because they breached their covenant, We cursed them and made their hearts grow hard. They changed the words from their context and forgot a part of the message sent to them. You will not cease to find deceit among them, except for a few. Forgive them and overlook their misdeeds! For Allah loves those who are kind.

Once again, the accusation of deception in this third statement—similar to the previous ones—does not apply to Christians. The sentence "They changed the words from their context and forget a part of the message sent to them" indicates a biased interpretation arrived at by removing the message from its primary purpose, not by means of a falsification of the text.

The fourth and final use of *ḥarrafa* presents a similar pattern:

Al-Mā'idah 5:41

> 41 O Messenger! Do not be saddened by those who hasten into unbelief by pretending to be believers with their lips while their hearts have no faith, nor by those among the Jews who pay attention to every lie and listen to others who have never come to you. They change the words from their context and say, "If you are told so, accept it. If not, be careful!" Those who think to be able to escape Allah's punishment would know that they have no protection against Him. These cannot expect Allah to purify their hearts. For them, there is disgrace in this world and a heavy punishment in the Hereafter.

Again, the reproach formulated here is addressed to "*some* among the Jews" and *not* to the Christians. It does not suggest any change in the content but a misinterpretation of the text due to a lack of consideration for the context.

In conclusion:

- The reproach of "changing something" (taḥrif) is addressed to Jews only and, therefore, concerns the Old Testament (Taurat and Zabur). The New Testament (Injil) is not implicated.

- The reproach concerns "some of them." If only "some of them" had changed the text, the others would have kept the proper text; so there would be two Bibles today. Yet there is only one.

The "Notarization" of the Honored Bible

Did the Honored Quran invalidate the previous books? If so, should the Honored Taurat, Zabur, and Injil be put aside? Are those books like the first telephone 140 years ago, while the Honored Quran would be like the newest smartphone? Our study has not identified any single ayah attesting to such an affirmation; on the contrary! Consider how many quranic ayat express the concept of "confirmation":

- Al-Baqarah 2:41, 89, 91, 101
- An-Nisā' 4:47
- Al-Mā'idah 5:48
- Al-An'ām 6:92
- Al-Fāṭir 35:31
- Al-Aḥqāf 46:12, 30, etc.

Generally translated with "to confirm," the Arabic word *muṣaddiqan* refers to the legalization of a document.[11] Consequently, we may compare the "confirmation" of the Honored Bible with the work of a clerk. This excludes any possibility of falsification. If no diligent lawyer would consent to legalize a fake document, how would the Honored Quran declare the Honored Bible a reliable document if it was a forgery? May Allah forbid! The use of *muṣaddiqan* takes away all suspicion about the validity of the former revelations; in other words, the Honored Quran did not come to *correct* but to *confirm* the Honored Bible's validity.

Some claim that Constantine the Great is the one who altered the Honored Bible. Notice that the Roman Emperor lived over 300 years *before* the compilation of the quranic canon. The Honored Quran was given *after* "the clear statement made to the people in the Book" (Al-Baqarah 2:159). That explains why all those affirmations are in the present tense, implying that they refer to the Honored Bible as it was available at the time of the compilation of the Honored Quran. Therefore, the claim of corruption cannot be applied to Constantine.

11 It is also used nowadays for the certification of organic food.

Others object that the text of the Honored Bible was altered *afterward.* Technically speaking, such an action is hardly conceivable. When the Honored Quran confirmed the veracity of the Honored Bible, Christianity had already spread in vast areas of Africa, Asia, and Europe. In that case, the following questions must be answered:

- *When* and *where* in history have Christians worldwide agreed upon the changes to be made in their Holy Texts and accepted them?
- *Where* is the list of such changes?
- *Who* are the forgers who did this? Can someone give names?
- *How* could Jews and Christians have agreed to corrupt the texts about Jesus (piuh) as the Messiah when the Jews are still rejecting his messianicity?
- *How* could Jews and Christians have collected and destroyed all the thousands of copies already in circulation worldwide?
- *How* could all those who owned a copy of the authentic Bible be convinced to exchange it for a corrupted version?
- *How* is it that no one protested? How could the Muslim 'Umma have accepted such a blasphemous action?
- *How* is it imaginable that no one has kept one single copy of the genuine text?
- *Why* hasn't the Muslim world saved any copy of the accurate Bible?
- *Why* didn't the Jews and Christians who embraced Islam retain their original Scriptures (especially those foretelling the coming of Muhammad (pbuh))?
- *Who* could have benefitted from the falsification?
- *What* sense would it have made to Jews and Christians to corrupt their books and to refuse a correcting revelation?
- If the original Bible had contained prophecies about Muhammad (pbuh), Jews and Christians would have spared themselves much trouble by simply accepting the message of Muhammad (pbuh) and by embracing Islam!
- *Why* did so many Christians suffer discrimination in the Middle Ages or during the time of communism for the sake of a religious book that had been allegedly falsified?

If you consider possible answers, you will quickly realize that the claim of falsification *after* the Honored Quran was composed can only be considered a highly implausible hypothesis without any historical foundation.

The Contribution of Archaeology

The most solid argument in favor of the credibility of the Honored Bible is that the text used for the current translations was written between 390 and 405 AD; i.e., *before* the Honored Quran. Consequently, the Honored Quran confirms the text we have in our hands.

Indeed, another way to support the validity of the Honored Bible has been provided by archaeology. Due to the search for witnesses to the past, people became passionate about ancient artifacts and began to dig in the sands of the deserted areas of the Middle East. Why the Orient? Westerners thought that it was the place where civilization began—and they were not wrong.

Among the most remarkable discoveries of archaeology, I should refer to nearly 24,000 early portions of the Honored Bible found in tombs, the recesses of some flea markets, and the basements of ancient monasteries. These texts written on stones, clay tablets, papyri, or parchments are much older than the samples of the Honored Bible that have been circulating for centuries.

Interestingly, the oldest part of the Honored Taurat ever found is 2,200 years old. Discovered in Egypt, it contains the holy Ten Commandments given to Musa (pbuh) by Allah Himself, as well as the Jewish confession of faith stating Allah's oneness.

In 1947 a young shepherd threw stones in different directions to find the goat he had lost. Suddenly, little Muhammad, as his name was, heard an unusual sound. So he decided to climb the hill with his cousins Jum'a Muhammad and Khalil Musa to identify the origin of the strange noise. Indeed, the stones had hit old jars hidden in a cave close to the top. These contained scrolls of the Honored Taurat, written by hand—one over seven meters long and nearly one thousand years older than all translations in circulation.

For the scholars in charge of deciphering these ancient documents, the most immense excitement was felt at the chance to compare them with the Taurat that Jews and Christians already had in their hands. To what extent would the two texts differ?

To their amazement, they established an almost perfect transmission of the text throughout the centuries. Only very insignificant details differed. No wonder the discovery shocked those who had been rejecting the accuracy of the Honored Bible.

“To their amazement, they established an almost perfect transmission of the text throughout the centuries.”

Concerning the Honored Injil, the oldest portion found so far is a papyrus dated 125 AD,[12] with a portion of the Gospel of John, Chapter 18, verses 37, 38:

> 37 "(I have come into the world) to bear witness to the Truth."
> 38 Pilate asked him: "What is truth?"

The abundance of manuscripts demonstrates that the text has been transmitted with accuracy. That is why Sir Frederic Kenyon, paleographer, president of the British Academy, and director of the British Museum, declared, "The Bible is the best-preserved antique book we possess" (Kenyon 1940, p. 132). Indeed, we only have one manuscript for most classical authors, such as Homer or Aristotle, and these are much younger than the originals. Still, no one would dare challenge their validity.

Some object that there are significant discrepancies between editions in use, and they are right. However, this issue is a matter of translation variations, which do *not* affect the reliability of the Hebrew, Aramaic, and Greek texts.

More Reasons to Doubt?

The arguments in favor of a change are primarily pragmatic. For instance, you may have heard Muslims say that texts announcing the coming of Muhammad (pbuh) have been erased from the Honored Injil. Paradoxically, the proponents of this idea are the first to quote the Honored Injil to apply the promise of a "Comforter"[13] to their Messenger (pbuh) and to claim that he is still mentioned in the text we have. In that case, they cannot simultaneously pretend that the text we have in our hands has been falsified by taking away the texts about Muhammad (pbuh), and also quote them! Accepting the validity of some texts—the ones that fit into their conception—and considering others as corrupted implies that those who changed the Honored Bible did not work thoroughly. In that case, there must be some truth in the Honored Bible to be still accepted as reliable and, therefore, to be followed.

Another source of hesitation is that the Honored Injil contains four Gospels and several epistles written by the apostles. Curiously, those who reject the Honored Bible because of this plurality are quick to assert the existence of a fifth Gospel, allegedly written by the Apostle Barnabas.

---

12 Papyrus P^{52}. Its discovery in Egypt and the fact that it is dated thirty years after the original (which was written in Ephesus, Asia Minor) indicates the importance given to this text and its wide circulation.

13 The Aramaic word *mənaḥem* being (erroneously) confused with the name *Muham-mad.*

The answer is that the Honored Quran repeats the same story in different words.[14] Variations between accounts of one event do not necessarily mean that they *contradict* each other. Instead, they may be complementary; like two loudspeakers playing different sounds and forming a powerful musical experience (called "stereo").

Some have identified slight mistakes in grammar and wording, as well as some contradictions. The question is whether inspiration is affected by slight mistakes. As long as the core message remains intact, the answer is no. Imagine you find an ancient parchment resembling a map. Looking attentively, you realize it shows the way to a hidden treasure. If it is worn and scratched, even if one part is missing, would you throw it away? I hope not! Instead, you would try to decode its mysterious instructions and follow them until you find the treasure.

Therefore, why don't you study what the Honored Quran calls "Guidance and Light"? Then you will be able to decide whether it convinces you or not.

Theological Divergences Between the Sacred Books

Another argument for questioning the validity of the Honored Bible lies in the theological divergences between the Books. The most apparent concerns Jesus (piuh) and the oneness of Allah. The last chapter of this book will clarify this issue.

Having studied the Honored Bible and the Honored Quran for nearly forty years and with as few preconceptions as possible, I conclude that the message of both books is much more similar than many would ever imagine.[15] Again, we should emphasize the common ground rather than the dissimilarities!

Finally, one may argue that some Christians discredit their Holy Book or do not treat it with much respect. Such a lack of reverence is disturbing but does not prove any falsification.

Therefore, we should be cautious not to restrict our horizons to our elbows—what we have learned at school, from our environment, or from the media! Let us instead take time to study the Honored Bible by

---

14 One example is the story of Adam and Eva (pbut), found in Al-Baqarah 2, Al-A'rāf 7, and Ṭā-Hā 20. I invite you to compare the three surat by yourself.

15 I have published several comparative studies between the Sacred Books. You will find more information at the end of this book.

ourselves! Then we can decide whether these books are beneficial or not. That is what the Honored Quran tells us in ʻĀli ʻImrān 3:3, 4:

> 3 He has sent down to you the Book with truth, confirming what was before it. He has previously sent down Taurat and Injil,
> 4 As a Guidance for mankind. He has sent down the Furqān.[16] Those who cover the Signs of Allah will suffer the severest penalty, and Allah is exalted in might, Lord of retribution.

Hudan: a Guidance to Mankind

The word *hudan* (guidance) is—at least partly—connected to the daily prayer *Ih'dinā as-ṣirāṭ al-mus'taqīm* ("Guide us into the Right Way"). In other words, if you want to find the Right Way, then read the Honored Bible!

Again the word *hudan* appears, this time regarding both the Honored Taurat and the Honored Injil. Several quranic ayat introduce the Honored Bible as a "guidance," applying the word *hudan* to "those who are God-conscious," such as in Surah Al-Mā'idah 5:46:

> 46 We have sent Isa ibn Maryam in their footsteps, confirming what was in his hands from the Taurat. We gave him the Injil, guidance, and light, confirming what was in his hands from the Taurat, a guidance and an admonition to the God-conscious.

No one will earnestly pretend that the "God-conscious" are only the Jews and the Christians. This appellation *must* include the Muslim world, and that is why Surah Al-Aḥqāf 46:30 adds:

> 30 They said, "O our people! We have heard a Book sent down after Musa, confirming what came before it. It guides us into the Truth and the Right Way.

Rejecting such authentic ("confirmed") guidance into the Truth would be foolish. It would be like turning off GPS navigation in an unknown area or turning away a bedouin who knows the desert in which you are lost. Moreover, this is not just about a nice walk but about eternal life.

16 *Al-Furqān* (the distinction) may be understood as the Honored Quran or as the Holy Ten Commandments given by Allah to Musa (pbuh).

Conclusion of Chapter 2

The belief in the validity of all the earliest revelations of Allah is part of the creed of Islam. It implies that all Muslims are to believe in the Honored Bible, where the verb "to believe" means to read and to follow. Consequently, whoever does not implement the teachings of the previous Books in his or her life has "truly drifted away."

An-Nisā' 4:136

> 136 O you who believe! Believe in Allah and His Messenger, in the Book He has sent down to His Messenger, and in the Book He has previously sent down. Whoever hides (something) about Allah, His angels, His Scriptures, His Messengers, and the Day After has lost his way and drifted away.

Therefore, each one must ask himself:

- *How* can the Honored Quran command believers to believe in a book if it were no longer available in the Honored Quran's time?
- *How* can someone profess to believe in a book and declare simultaneously that it has been falsified?
- *How* can someone say: "I believe" in a book if he does not read it, meditate upon it, or apply it to his or her life?
- *Why* do we not scrutinize a book that is supposed to be a reliable road map for our eternal destiny?

Back to the question asked at the beginning: which part of the Honored Bible has been falsified? The answer is: not a single one! On the contrary, our study has brought us to the discovery that neither the Honored Quran, nor the Hadiths (early exegetes of the Quran), nor the *mufassirūn* express the slightest suspicion toward the authenticity of the Honored Taurat, Zabur, and Injil.

That is why it is hard to understand why so many believers claim that the Honored Bible has been distorted and why they direct such severe criticism against it! My friends, the matter is too serious to be fueled by preconceived ideas. Therefore, I invite you to investigate the facts for yourself. I can only encourage you to follow the advice of scholars like Al-Bāqillānī and Al-Ġazālī: to take the Honored Bible in your hand and study it on your own!

Furthermore, in case you still have some hesitation about it, I encourage you to listen to the words of the Honored Quran:

Yūnus 10:94

> 94 If you have any doubt concerning what We have sent down to you, ask those who read the Book before you. The Truth comes from your Lord. Therefore, do not be among those who doubt.

May I take the above ayah as an invitation to test the integrity of all books? If you cherish its advice and study the content of the Honored Bible, there will be no more excuse to distrust the Truth.

Instead of disputing without rationale, let us face the evidence and eradicate once and for all the severe accusations of corruption of the Honored Bible! There is no ground to support those claims. On the contrary, the Honored Quran Itself commands believers to profess belief in the former Scriptures. In other words, reading and obeying the godly revelations in the Honored Bible should be considered an essential part of what makes you a genuine Muslim.

Therefore, no one can assume that the Honored Bible has been annulled through the sending of the Honored Quran. Woe to him who believes and spreads falsehood. Whoever treats Allah's revelations in such a way blasphemes the Omniscient (al-ʿAlīm) and Guardian (al-Ḥafīẓ) over His Word. Is it conceivable that the very reproach that Muhammad (pbuh) directed against Jews and Christians of his time ("they forgot a part of what they were supposed to remember") may also apply to some of us today?

Al-Mā'idah 5:14

> 14 We made a covenant with those who call themselves Chris-tians, but they forgot a part of what they were supposed to re-member from it. We aroused enmity and hatred between them until the Resurrection Day. Soon, Allah will show them what they have done.

Could it be that some reject something they have never thoroughly analyzed by themselves? It takes courage to fight prejudices. But this is a necessary step toward deep knowledge. Therefore, I invite you to read the Honored Bible and form your opinion. Are you ready to make the effort to study Allah's revelation thoroughly and carefully? If yes, you will find a great treasure for your life.

I have written this book after investigating the former Scriptures, and I can confirm that these Books are from Allah!

Reading the Honored Quran, we discover the names of prophets and messengers listed without more detailed information about them. It could indicate that those who listened to Muhammad (pbuh) knew the stories and words of these prophets and messengers (pbut) from the older Scriptures.

To learn more about the prophets and messengers (pbut) mentioned in the Honored Quran, we only have to read the Honored Bible. In it, you will find detailed stories of Adam/Adam, Noah/Nuḥ, Abraham/Ibrahim and his sons Isaac/Isḥaq and Ishmael/Ishmael; Jacob/Yaqub and his son Joseph/Yusuf, Musa, David/Dawud and his son Solomon/Sulaiman, Elijah/Ilyas, Jonah/Yunus, John the Baptist/Yaḥya Ibn Zakariya (pbut), and his cousin Jesus /Al-Masih Isa Ibn Maryam (piuh).

Therefore, if you are convinced that the Honored Quran and Islamic tradition are on our side, you can confidently trust the existing "road map" provided by the All-Wise and Omniscient. If some parts are hard to understand or to apply in your life, do not worry too much! Keep searching! Be persevering. As the Arab proverb says: "Perseverance is the key to success."

- Let us stop trusting those doubters who discredit the Honored Bible.
- Let us stop listening to those who call themselves "believers" but do not live according to the Scriptures of their religion.
- Let us implore Allah to guide us as He has promised in Al-Baqarah 2:186:

> 186 When my servants ask you about Me, tell them I am near. I answer the invocation of the supplicant who calls Me. Therefore, let them hear My call and trust Me so they might be rightly guided.

Some Verses from the Honored Bible

Related to Chapter 2

Taurat, Jeremiah 29:12-14a

12 You will call me and pray to me, and I will hear you.

13 You will seek me and find me, having done so from the heart.

14 And I'll let you find me.

Taurat, Jeremiah 33:3

3 Call me and I'll answer. I'll show you great things you can't even imagine.

Taurat, 2nd Samuel 12:9a

9 Why have you despised the word of the Lord by doing what is vile in his sight?

Taurat, Proverbs 30:5

5 Every word emanating from God is impeccable; He is a shield to those who take refuge in him.

Taurat, Isaiah 40:8

8 Grass withers and flowers fall, but God's word endures forever.

Taurat, Jeremiah 1:12

12 You have seen correctly because I'm watching over my word to be sure that it's fulfilled.

Zabur, Psalm 33:4

4 The word of the Lord is accurate. God is faithful in everything He does.

Zabur, Psalm 119:105, 162

105 Your word is a lamp to my feet and a light to my path.

162 I enjoy your commandments like someone who has found a great treasure.

Injil, Gospel of Luke 11:28

28 Blessed are those who hear God's word and put it into practice.

Injil, Gospel of John 7:17

17 He who chooses to do God's will determines whether my teaching comes from God or whether I speak on my own.

Injil, Gospel of John 8:32, 47

32 You will discover the truth, and the truth will set you free.

47 Whoever belongs to God hears what he says. You do not hear because you do not belong to him.

Injil, Gospel of John 13:19

19 I'm telling you this before it happens, so that when it does, you'll believe it's me.

Injil, Gospel of John 17:17

17 Sanctify them with the truth; your word is the truth.

Injil, 1st Epistle of Peter 1:23, 24

24 All men are like grass, and all their glory is like the flowers of the field; the grass withers, and the flowers fall,

25 But the word of the Lord remains unchanged forever, and this is the word that was preached to you as good news.

Injil, Epistle of Paul to the Hebrews 4:12

12 God's word is life-giving and effective, sharper than a two-edged sword, separating soul and spirit by penetrating ligament and marrow; it challenges the feelings and thoughts of the heart.

بسم الله الرحمن الرحيم

Chapter 3

The Blessed Feast Eid al-Adha

Dear brothers and sisters, let us exalt Allah the Glorious for His goodness toward us!

Al-Hašr 59:23, 24

23 He is Allah. Besides Him, there is no other God. He is the Sovereign Lord, the Holy One, the Source of security, the Keeper of Faith, the Guardian, the Mighty One, the All-Powerful, the Proud! Exalted be He above all the partners they ascribe to Him.

24 He is Allah, the Creator, the Originator, and the Shaper out of nothing. His are the most beautiful names. All that is in heaven and earth glorifies Him. He is the Mighty and the Wise.

This chapter is an invitation to meditate on what the Honored Quran says about the Blessed Feast Eid al-Adha. Let us share some considerations about that heartbreaking event to appreciate it better and teach our children to do so. Recalling the narrative around Ibrahim's son, the Honored Quran says:

Aṣ-Ṣāffāt 37:107

107 We ransomed him with a tremendous sacrifice.

A Shocking Command

Opening the pages of the Honored Quran, we read about a prophet who occupies a unique rank. He is called by an unusual name: "Allah's friend." This prophet is our master Ibrahim (pbuh).

An-Nisā' 4:125

125 Who is better in religion than he who fully submits to Allah while doing good and following the state of mind of Ibrahim, the upright in faith? Allah chose him as a friend.

"Allah's friend"—what an unusual name for a human! It expresses a particular relationship with Allah. A friend is someone to whom you can tell everything and ask anything. Indeed, Allah the Wise trusted Ibrahim (pbuh) as you may count on someone you know. That might explain why Allah asked him one day to perform such a shocking act: sacrificing his son. Let us read together the whole narrative in Surah Aṣ-Ṣāffāt 37:102-107!

102 Then, when (the son) reached (the age of) (serious) work with him, he said: "O my son! I see in vision that I offer you: Now see what your view is!" (The son) said: "O my father! Do as you are commanded. If Allah wills, you will find me practicing patience and constancy."

103 So when they had both submitted their will, and he had laid him prostrate on his forehead,

104 We called out to him, "O Ibrahim!

105 You have already fulfilled the vision!" Indeed, We reward those who do right in this way.

106 For this was a trial.

107 And We ransomed him with a tremendous sacrifice.

These ayat disclose a dialogue between Allah and Prophet Ibrahim (pbuh). Not only did the Sovereign King talk to a human being, but He gave him the most challenging command any mortal person has ever been asked to obey—an order that is hard to understand. Allah spoke to Ibrahim (pbuh) in a dream, asking him to take his beloved son to a hill and offer him there to Him.

Some argue that the Honored Quran does not mention anything about Allah telling Ibrahim (pbuh) to kill his son. They say that the patriarch had a vision in which he saw himself slaughtering his son. The Honored Quran never explicitly says that the dream was from Allah. However, Ibrahim (pbuh) interpreted it as a divine command.

Submission Implies Obedience

Let us try for a moment to imagine Ibrahim (pbuh) awakening his sleeping son in the darkness of the dawn and whispering the command to get up and go on a journey with him. It takes them several days, and Ibrahim's heart is his heaviest burden ever. The patriarch calls on Allah's compassion to change His will every night. However, no answer comes to cancel what the prophet has heard. Allah is the Eternal, Absolute, and Self-Sufficient. He never changes His verdicts.

Eventually, Ibrahim (pbuh) sees the hill indicated in the dream. The young man probably wonders where a sacrificial animal is:

"Father!"

"Yes, my son?"

"I can see that you have the coals and the wood, but tell me, where is the lamb?"

Please close your eyes! Can you see the old man and his son walking side by side? Observe how they build an altar and arrange the wood on it! First, the patriarch turns his face away. His cherished son should not see the tears rolling down his cheeks. Finally, he tells his son what Allah, the Irresistible One, has commanded.

Can you feel the horror felt by the young man? The child is strong enough to overpower his father and run away. He wonders how Allah could ask something that, at first glance, looks typically pagan.

However, after Ibrahim (pbuh) explains everything, the boy agrees. He shares his father's faith. He willingly submits—the most remarkable attitude of piety ever witnessed in any human being!

The father's devotion is perfectly reflected and equaled by the son's. Ibrahim (pbuh) loved Allah so much that he gave his son, and the son so loved Allah and his father that he gave himself to Him! Indeed, the world has never seen such a demonstration of affection, such wholehearted surrender to Allah, the Greatest, on the part of a human father and his child.

Both eventually embrace in a last goodbye, their hearts bleeding with sorrow. The old father ties the lad and lays him on the altar. While calling on Allah's mercy with a loud "*Bismillah*[17]," he grasps and raises the knife, ready to cut the throat of his beloved son.

---

17 The basmalla is an invocation of the name of God, often used before praying, travelling, eating, or, in this case, making a sacrifice.

Divine Intervention

Someone may ask whether Allah has the right to demand such a sacrifice. Of course, Allah has all rights! Nevertheless, Allah has compassion for Ibrahim (pbuh) and his son. At that very moment, as the old man lifts his knife to kill his son, an angel appears and stops him. Suddenly, Ibrahim (pbuh) hears a voice calling out from heaven:

"Ibrahim!"

He answers, "Yes, here I am."

"Don't hurt the lad or do anything to him. Now I know that you have obedient reverence for Allah because you have not kept back your only son from him."

Ibrahim (pbuh) looks around and sees a ram caught in a bush by its horns. He takes it and offers it instead of his son.

The Meaning

Aṣ-Ṣāffāt 37:107

107 We ransomed him with a tremendous sacrifice.

"We ransomed him" or, in a more explicit translation, "We made an animal chosen to rescue him and spared him from slaughter." This phenomenal story has made a considerable impression on millions of minds worldwide. Since it is the origin of the Blessed Feast Eid al-Adha—the central event in the Islamic calendar—let us ponder it for a moment:

- Who had to die? Either Ibrahim's son or a ram had to die.
- What was a lonesome ram doing on the top of a mountain? It was indeed a miraculous appearance!
- Where did the animal come from? It came from Allah.
- Who gave it? Allah gave it.
- Who was slaughtered? The animal was slaughtered.
- Who stayed alive? Ibrahim's son stayed alive.

Please consider that Ibrahim (pbuh) probably owned thousands of sheep and could have offered them *all* to Allah. Ibrahim (pbuh) is called "the upright in faith" and "truly submitted to Allah." Despite such a remarkable attitude of submission, one can imagine his natural reaction:

> "My Lord, I was so afraid for my son. I love him more than all my possessions. Why did You let me suffer so terribly with such a command? And then, as I finally arrived on the mountain, You gave me an animal to kill. Why didn't You tell me that it is what You wanted? I would have gladly slaughtered *hundreds* of rams for You and given my whole flock to You!"

Allah, though, would have answered Ibrahim's objection (pbuh) by saying something like:

> "Ibrahim, my friend, I know how much you cherish your son. But all your riches and flocks would not be sufficient to release your son. Only *one* thing is of higher value than your flesh, and only *one* thing can save the young man from death: *my* ram, the one I have chosen! And *I am giving it to you*!"

I wonder why Allah asked His "friend" to forfeit his son rather than some other possession. The reason is that there was and could be nothing more treasured to a man than his son. Yet Ibrahim's submission to Allah was even more significant than his love for his son.

Furthermore, Allah would probably say:

> "*The only one* who is worth more than your son, the only one who can die instead of your son, is *my ram*. And I give it to you as a gift from Heaven. Even if you do not understand everything, accept it!"

> Of course, Ibrahim (pbuh) could have rejected Allah's gift. He could have said:

> "Oh no, my Lord, I cannot accept such a great gift. I do not want you to bring such a tremendous present for me."

But if he had done so, what would have happened then? The answer would be pretty straightforward:

"All right, my friend, but if you do not want to kill my ram, you must execute your son. He must die, for this is my command."

Is the situation clear? Think about it!

- Either the ram that comes from Allah stays alive, but then the son of Ibrahim (pbuh) has to die,
- Or the ram from Allah dies, and the son can stay alive.

A Matter of Life and Death

What did our Ibrahim (pbuh) decide? He obeyed Allah so that his son could live. He accepted that the ram should die instead of his son. He was fully subjected to Allah's will—and that is why he is called "the father of all who surrender to Allah" as we read in the Honored Quran in 'Āli 'Imrān 3:67:

> 67 Ibrahim was neither a Jew nor a Christian but was an upright man who had surrendered to Allah. He was not of the idol worshipers.

> "Ibrahim (pbuh) was fully subjected to Allah's will, and ... is called "the father of all who surrender to Allah.""

Each one who claims to be a *muslim* ("submitting" to Allah) must follow the way of our master Ibrahim (pbuh):

- It is not his good deeds that will demonstrate his consent to surrender,
- But his acceptance of the lamb provided by Allah.

Everyone who celebrates Eid al-Adha commemorates the precious sacrifice that came from Allah. Like the ram that Ibrahim (pbuh) slaughtered, every animal killed during the Blessed Feast symbolizes what Allah has provided.

But does Allah have a flock of sheep in Heaven? Surely not! Instead, Allah wanted to show His friend Ibrahim (pbuh) that He was willing to provide a gift called *'aẓīm*, of great value and significance, so that his son (pbuh) might stay alive.

Therefore, I can only wonder how much Allah loves His creatures. How merciful He is! Allah gave something pure enough, like a ram—something precious, sufficient to redeem Ibrahim's son from death.

However, the question remains unanswered: Why did Allah ask for such an act and then give an animal instead of a child? Did He want to test Ibrahim's ability (pbuh) to subject himself to Him?

I should add that Allah Himself provided the sacrificial ram. If Allah only wanted to test His friend, why did an animal die instead of his son? There must be a deeper meaning.

How it All Began

To understand the true significance of this unique story, let us go back to the beginning of human history. The Holy Books introduce Allah as the Creator of all things:

Al-Baqarah 2:117

117 Originator of the heavens and the earth: When He decrees a thing, He merely says, "Be!" And it is.

Al-A'rāf 7:54

54 Truly, your Lord is Allah, who created the heavens and the earth in six days, then was established upon the throne.
He covers the night with the day and makes the sun and the stars subservient by His command. His is all creation and commandment. Blessed be Allah, the Lord of the worlds!

Then, it is said that Allah formed Adam (pbuh), breathed His spirit into him, and placed him in the garden of Eden/'Adn with his wife Eve/Eva (pbuh).

Al-Ḥiğr 15:28, 29

28 And (remember) when your Lord said to the angels, "I am creating man of the clay of molded mud.
29 When I have shaped and breathed My spirit into him, kneel and prostrate yourselves before him!"

The Honored Quran states that Allah made Adam (pbuh) responsible for the Garden of 'Adn. He was the steward of Allah's creation. The Arabic word used to express the position given to Adam (pbuh) is *khalifa* (caliph).

Al-Baqarah 2:30

30 Recall when your Lord told the angels, "I am setting a man (Adam) on the earth as a steward." They asked, "Will you put one that will work maliciously and shed blood when we praise and sanctify your name?" He (Allah) answered, "Surely I know what you know not."

Adam and Eva (pbut) were honored in a particular way:

- Allah communicated with them.
- Thus, they were honored with a close relationship with Him.
- They were honored to live in the best environment one can imagine.
- They were honored by being appointed caliph over Allah's creation.
- They were honored by the ability to obey or disobey.
- They were honored by a state of absolute purity.

How generous is Allah, the Beneficent! He is *Rabb ul 'ālamīn*, the Lord of the universe, Creator, and Sustainer of everything. He is the Provider and the Gentle One. He is the Source of goodness, so merciful that He nurtures all animals and birds without arbitrary preference. How much more does He care for every human? Allah gave Adam (pbuh) a splendid orchard with everything in abundance. Adam (pbuh) had all the food he wanted; he did not need to work hard. He was indeed filled with joy and gratitude.

Imagine a rich and powerful landlord. One day, he comes to a beggar and says:

"Sir, you look so miserable. You do not even wear a decent shirt. Come and stay in my villa. Various trees surround it: figs, oranges, mangoes, peaches, and others. All this now is yours. So, feel at home, help yourself, and enjoy!"

Wouldn't that poor man be happy?

But suppose the landlord established only one restriction, such as:

"Yes, you can eat from every tree—except for a single one, that one over there. Please do not pick its fruits!"

Don't you think the man would be so grateful that he would gladly do anything for that landlord, including not touching *one* specific tree? Of course, he would!

But what if this man disobeyed and ate from that fruit? What would the landlord do, and how would he feel?

That is precisely what happened. Allah is the Source of serenity, safety, and blessings. He is the Guardian and the Protector. He, the supreme Teacher, warned our first parents against the snares of Iblīs, because He intended to protect them.

> "Allah warned our first parents against the snares of Iblīs, because He intended to protect them."

Al-A'rāf 7:19

> 19 Then Allah commanded, "O Adam! Dwell you and your wife in the Garden, and enjoy (eating from good things) as you wish. But do not come near to this tree, lest you become wrongdoers."

Ṭā-Hā 20:115

> 115 We have made a covenant with Adam before, but he forgot, and we found no firm resolve on his part.

The word translated as "We made a covenant" is *'ahid'nā*. It is the same in Surah Al-Fātiḥah, where the believers ask Allah for "guidance into the Right Way." In other words, Allah had given Adam and Eva (pbut) enough advice for them to stay on the Right Way. The "guidance" was a clear warning against Iblīs, the master of deception and enemy of Allah and man:

Ṭā Hā 20:117

[117] Then We said, "O Adam, assuredly this Shaytan is an enemy to you and your wife, so let him not drive you both out of the Garden, lest you plunge into affliction."

Indeed, Shaytan misled Adam and Eva (pbut):

Ṭā Hā 20:120, 121

[120] But Shaytan whispered maliciously to him, saying, "O Adam, shall I show you the tree of immortality and a kingdom that never decays?"

[121] They both ate of its fruit, so their nakedness appeared to them. They began to cover themselves with leaves from the Garden. Thus, Adam disobeyed his Lord and went astray.

Some people play down the first transgression to the level of forgetfulness. However, remember that Adam and Eva (pbut) had been created without any fault. In Islam, *fitra* is the inborn desire to serve Allah. It is the ability to know Him, to be loyal to Him, and to worship Him in the Right Way.

The word "to disobey" used in Ayah 121 is *'asāyi*; it may be translated as "to resist," "oppose," or "defy." That implies that the disobedience of Adam (pbuh) was not just a tiny mistake or a misstep. It was a breach of trust in Allah's goodness and omniscience. Shaytan had promised Adam and Eva (pbut) "immortality and a kingdom that never decays." Therefore, the temptation was for them to become proud like he was. Listening to him meant succumbing to the desire to become like Allah. By reaching out and eating the forbidden fruit, Adam and Eva (pbut) outwardly expressed their rebellion against Allah. They became Shaytan's allies in his revolt. The desire to become someone higher than what they had been created for was the cause of Shaytan's fall and the decline of humanity.

Therefore, this act must be considered an act of outward disobedience that reflects Shaytan's and man's hearts:

Al-Kahf 18:50

[50] And (remember) when We said to the angels, "Prostrate yourselves before Adam," all prostrated themselves, except Shaytan. He was of the jinn and rebelled against his Lord's command. Will you then choose him and his offspring for your protecting friends instead of Me despite their hostility toward you? Calamity is the result of wrongdoing.

Al-Ḥajj 22:3

> 3 And among the people, some dispute about Allah without knowledge, and they follow every rebellious devil.

Thus, the Honored Quran blames our first parents for eating the fruit. It was an act of conscious rebellion.

What is Sin?

Sin is more than an outward sign of disobedience. It is distrust of Allah's goodness. Such an attitude reflects the desire to rise above our status as limited creatures.

Because there is only one God, desiring to be "like the Most High" is equal to wishing to push Him off His holy throne and take His place. Whoever steals, lies, or cheats tries to justify himself by accusing the victim of being bad enough to deserve our wrongdoing.

Sin is the execution of a verdict. The problem is we seldom consider ourselves worthy of punishment, and we are likely to perceive our transgressions with our self-made pair of "after all" glasses. We say (or at least think), "*After all*, the shop owner is asking too much money"; "*After all*, he does not treat his employees correctly"; "*After all*, he has sold me some bad products in the past"; "… and all of that gives me the right to cheat him." It is the same for whomever who wants to be unfaithful: "*After all*, my partner is not as she or he should be; does not do as she or he should"; and at that stage, the unfaithful one finds 1,000 excuses to cheat on his or her spouse.

Humans are generally quick to allow themselves to formulate their own definition of justice, as if they were a jury acting on behalf of the rest of humanity.

We may conclude that the transgression of Adam and Eva (pbut) was due to their self-given right to decide that Allah was unfair. As such, their act was a sign of their rebellion against Him. Therefore, it could by no means remain without consequences. Allah had to convince humans that their transgression was not excusable.

We also know that Allah had clearly warned Adam (pbuh) that if he disobeyed, he and his wife would have to leave the Garden.

The ultimate and logical consequence of such a rebellion is devastation, as the Honored Quran says:

Al-Baqarah 2:81

81 Whoever earns corruption and becomes surrounded in his sin shall be doomed to hell and dwell in it forever.

What is Death?

Death means the absence of life; it also implies the irreversible extinction of those who choose to reject Allah's signs. Let me suggest the following illustration:

- Imagine a spring watering an orchard. The life-giving liquid flows into a canal, filling it with freshness and purity. It grows many trees, vegetables, and flowers, making the garden look like paradise.
- But suppose someone stops up the canal. No water will run through the enclosure anymore. Without water, the beds will slowly dry up, and the vegetables and flowers will die.

This simple picture explains what happened to Adam and Eva (pbut): as long as they obeyed Allah, they received a wonderful and joyous existence from their Creator, for Allah is the Giver of energy—He *is* Life.

That is why, as soon as Adam and Eva (pbut) stopped following Allah's plan, their connection with Allah was interrupted; the channel between them and the source of life was blocked, and they began to die.

Al-Mu'minūn 23:99, 100

99 Finally, when death comes unto one of them, he says, "My Lord, send me back!

100 That I may do righteous deeds in what I had left undone," but it is only a word he speaks. Behind them is a barrier till the day they will be raised.

Take another example:

- A power station generates electricity. Your home has many electric wires through which energy can reach the various appliances and lights throughout the building.
- If you cut off ten meters from the wire, the electricity can no longer flow. The devices stop working, and the lights no longer shine.
- But what happens if you only make a tiny cut into the main electrical source cable with a razor blade? The result is the same: the power is off.

Regardless of the length of cable that has been cut off, the lights do not work.

So it is with our disobedience against Allah. Some moral failures may be appalling, while others may not. We naturally tend to minimize our wrongdoings, and that makes us instinctively think that we may escape the force of Allah's judgment. But the Honored Quran qualifies sin with many different words, thus showing how many faces badness may have. Some of them are used in the Honored Quran for severe acts of wickedness, such as the term *dhanab* (to commit a serious offense) or, in the case of an atrocious crime, *kabīra*.

Studying these different aspects will easily convince us that we are far from being *ṣāliḥ* (able to stand before Allah).

We might still wonder why disobedient humans would suffer such a terrible fate. After all, we are not all *that* bad! It is true that, from a human perspective, most of us may have done nothing to deserve being sentenced to death. But let us consider the other side: Which exemplary achievements have we done, if any, to have the right to live in this world and the next? Just as no human effort can create life, none can restore it.

Every heartbeat is an act of kindness from Allah. We have not done anything for it or deserved anything good from Him. We must realize that our whole lives are the product of divine care.

Allah's ninety-nine names express every aspect of purity. Allah is exempt from all weakness and wickedness, matchless in beauty and character. Nothing in this world and the world to come can be compared to Him because He is the Creator of everything.

Because Allah is holy, even what we may call the "smallest sin" is unbearable. Even the slightest corruption cannot stand in the presence of His incomparable purity. His wrath expresses the pain of seeing His perfect creation being damaged. That is why our first parents immediately felt ashamed and became afraid of Allah, the All-Seeing and All-Aware.

Whoever commits a moral mistake and suddenly realizes that Allah can see everything feels helpless. Suppose Allah wrote all your evil deeds and thoughts on a slate—maybe even a wall would not even be big enough—how would you feel? Embarrassed? Ashamed?

A Worldwide Pandemic

The Honored Quran describes the consequences of Adam and Eva's (pbut) rebellion as a pandemic that spread on our planet:

Al-Aʻrāf 7:24, 25

> [24] He said, "Go down (from hence), one of you a foe unto the other. You will have a habitation and provision on earth for a specific time.
> [25] There shall you live, and there shall you die. And from there, you will be brought forth."

Interestingly, the command "Go down from hence" only applied to Adam and Eva (pbut); the Arabic verb used in Ayah 24 should be in the so-called "dual form," which is a plural form used for only two individuals.[18] Indeed, the dual is used throughout the narration found in Surah Al-Aʻrāf. But suddenly, the command appearing here switches from dual to plural![19] It implies that the sentence does not concern only Adam and Eva (pbut). It implicates more than two people. This is not a coincidence. The Honored Quran emphasizes that the wrong decision taken by Adam and Eva (pbut) has affected all humankind. You and I no longer live in ʻAdn (Eden) but on a planet of suffering and vice.

Everyone can see that we humans have lost the honor Adam (pbuh) received as the caliph of the earth. Nature is no longer under our dominion except for a few domesticated animals. Despite scientists' most sophisticated inventions, storms, floods, and earthquakes are uncontrollable.

Now we realize that corruption is more than a matter of honor and shame; it is a matter of life and death. Like an epidemic, the rebellion against Allah immediately began to spread worldwide. There is no other explanation for why wickedness and death are universal. A proud and unbelieving person will not wish to acknowledge this sober truth that the Honored Bible discloses, but the world is filled with suffering.

Since the cause of misery on earth is found in the satanic law of egocentrism that reigns within every human being, no political party, no philosophical idea, not even religious dos and don'ts have the power to stop the spread of this universal tragedy. In case of a pandemic, as we have recently experienced, the only viable solution is that every malign virus must be eradicated; otherwise, it is just a matter of time before the whole body will be sick again. Think of the thousands of warnings signs and measures taken to stop such a pandemic! Likewise, if Allah does not eradicate sin, we are doomed. The result is that, sooner or later, the whole world will end up in an inferno of self-destruction.

---

18 In Arabic, dual is a plural form that applies to only two people or objects.
19 *baʻḍukum, walakum.*

In Surah An-Naḥl 16:61, we read:

> 61 If Allah was to punish men for their wrongdoing, He would not leave a single creature on earth, but He reprieves them to an appointed term, and when their term comes, they cannot put it back for a single hour, nor put it forward.

Good News Ahead!

The good news is that Allah did *not* give up on His creatures. Allah is not a judgmental God walking around with a rod. Allah hates sin, but He loves sinners. And that is why Allah took the first step toward Adam and Eva (pbut):

Al-A'rāf 7:22

> 22 Thus did he lead them by deceit; when they tasted of the tree, their shame was manifest to them, and they began to hide (by heaping) on themselves some of the leaves of the garden. And their Lord called them (saying), "Did I forbid you from that tree and tell you that assuredly Shaytan is an open enemy to you?"

I wonder why Allah asked Adam (pbuh) where he was. Don't you think He knew exactly where he was hiding? Of course He knew! Allah is the Omnipresent and Omniscient. Therefore, nothing can escape His eyes. But He wanted Adam and Eva (pbut) to realize how far they had rejected happiness. The first reaction of Adam and Eva (pbut) was to try to hide the problem and then fix it by themselves the best they could:

Ṭā Hā 20:121

> 121 They both ate of its fruit, and their nakedness appeared. They began to cover themselves with leaves. Thus, Adam disobeyed his Lord and went astray.

Acknowledging our wrongdoings has always been a humbling challenge. Instinctively, the human heart does not want to admit its failure. It prefers to accuse somebody else, including Allah, to justify itself. That is precisely what Adam and Eva (pbut) first did: because the disgrace seemed irreparable they did everything they could to hide it.

However, no self-made garment can hide our dishonor in front of Allah. Humans cannot create life, and none of us can repair it. In Allah's sight, the sinner is "naked." Allah knows every single thought. One thousand good acts that a person may do can never be good enough to make him or her eligible for Paradise. If Allah did not intervene, there would be no way out of such a disgrace.

Fortunately, Allah announced a way out:

Al-A‘rāf 7:25, 26

> 25 Allah said, “There shall you live, and there shall you die. From there, you will be brought forth.
> 26 Oh, children of Adam, We have sent down to you a raiment to conceal your shame and splendid vesture; but the cloth of righteousness, that is best. These are the signs of Allah, so they may remember.”

What happens here? A cloth came from Allah to cover the shame of Adam and Eva (pbut). Now they had no more reason to hide themselves from Allah’s sight. The connection was reestablished. Their disgrace was taken away; or, if you prefer, their dignity was restored. It means that on the very day when Adam and Eva (pbut) should have died, an animal was slaughtered, and its pelt was used to dress them. Thus, the shame of Adam and Eva (pbut) was covered with the fleece of the victim as a beautiful, new, and clean cloth. They did not need to feel disgraced before Allah or to hide anymore. Like the ram that died instead of Ibrahim’s son (pbuh), an animal coming from Allah protected their life.

“Like the ram that died instead of Ibrahim’s son (pbuh), an animal coming from Allah protected their life.”

Taqwāh

Allah Himself performed the first shedding of blood ever. He did it to provide skins that covered the nakedness of Adam and Eva (pbut). To make this happen, a living animal had to bleed and die instead of the sinners. Through its death, Adam and Eva (pbut) were released from sin and disgrace and acquitted of their sentence.

- The channel, which was blocked, is now reopened;
- The water begins to flow again;
- The garden is revived.

By the way, did you know that the Arabic verb *ghafara* (to forgive) also means “to protect” and “to watch over”? Its derivatives are used for meanings like “a scarf to cover the head” or “a helmet.” Interestingly, the Honored

Quran calls the robe given to those who turn to Allah *libāsut-taqwāh* (the cloth of righteousness)—an expression indicating that Allah's pardon is covering our infamy and, at the same time, protecting us from His verdict:

Al-A'rāf 7:26

26 Oh, children of Adam, yes, We have sent down a cloth to conceal your shame and splendid vesture, but the cloth of righteousness is best. These are the signs of Allah, so they may remember.

The sending of a cloth to conceal our shame applies to each of us. Surah Al-A'rāf 7:26 speaks to you and me. Here, Allah offers us His "righteousness," symbolized by a male sheep. Its death was necessary to restore our honor and reestablish the connection between Allah and us. It was not only essential but also sufficient: thanks to the death of this animal, there is no need to try to impress Allah by doing good actions. Our justification is achieved by Allah and not by man. Divine mercy, as revealed in the cloth of righteousness, is Allah's unexpected solution to the problem of sin and death. On the day of reckoning, those who accepted the cloth of righteousness will stand before Allah as if they had never rebelled. Their shame is covered, and they can enter the gates of Paradise. What excellent news!

Two Brothers—Two Choices

From the beginning, Allah has shown His prophets that He insists on blood. After the statement that Adam (pbuh) received *taqwāh* from Allah, we read of another instance where blood was shed, this time by Hābīl (pbuh). Adam's two sons, Cain/Qābīl and Abel/Hābīl (pbut) provided two very different kinds of sacrifices:

Al-Mā'idah 5:27

27 Recite to them with truth the story of the two sons of Adam, how they offered each a sacrifice, which was accepted by one and not by the other. The one said, "Surely I will kill you." "So what," the other said, "Allah accepts only from those who are righteous (*muttaqin*)."

The primary reason for a sacrifice is to bring Allah and man closer to each other. The Arabic word for "offering" is *qurbān*; it stems from *qaraba* (to get closer). It is sometimes used to describe the Blessed Feast, also called the "Qurbān Feast."

Many believers think they may come nearer to Allah through their offering. Qābīl brought his own "deeds"—the fruit he had gathered from his plot—and in the same way, many try to impress and manipulate Allah by bringing their good works as an offering. By acting so, they hope to earn access to eternal Paradise. However, Allah does not accept such gifts because none of them is suitable to bring us close to Allah:

Saba' 34:37

> 37 Not your wealth nor your children will bring you close to Us.

The above ayah affirms that no wealth, not even the gift of our children, could be acceptable to Allah as an appropriate *qurbān*.

No one can "buy" Allah's favor, no matter how significant his or her loss may be. A whole trainload of fruits and vegetables would not obtain forgiveness for even one sin. Qābīl was committing a grave mistake when he tried to fulfill Allah's covenant of promise through his planning and works.

There is no need to attempt to enter Paradise through the *bakshīsh* (bribe) of our exemplary accomplishments. Let us not be like Qābīl, the elder child of Adam (pbuh), who tried to hide his disgrace from Allah.

Al-Ḥajj 22:37

> 37 Note that neither their flesh nor blood, but your piety shall reach Allah. Has He subjugated them to you so that you should glorify Him for the guidance He has given you? And give glad tidings to the doers of good.

The above ayah exhorts us "Note it well!", thus introducing a unique lesson: Only our piety can reach Allah. Again, the word used here is *taqwāh*; and *taqwāh* is a blood sacrifice initiated by Allah and covering our shame as it happened with Adam (pbuh) and his son Hābīl (pbuh): They accepted the *taqwāh* sent down from Allah.

Hābīl (pbuh) offered one of the sheep from his flock, and Allah accepted it from him. By acting so, Hābīl followed the truth about *taqwāh* like his parents Adam and Eva (pbut) had done! Like Ibrahim (pbuh) centuries later, he subjected himself to Allah's will so that he could live: he accepted that a ram should die instead of the guilty one.

Therefore, our decision should be to follow the example of the patriarch and accept the most valuable gift that Allah has probably ever given. This is why Surah Hūd 11:3, 90 invites us:

> 3 Seek pardon from your Lord and turn to Him in repentance. He will give you fair enjoyment until an appointed term and will bestow His grace upon everyone who is graceful. But if you turn away, I fear the retribution of a mighty day for you.

[90] Ask for pardon from your Lord and turn to Him. For my Lord is indeed merciful, loving.

An-Nasr 110:3

[3] Celebrate the praise of your Lord and seek His forgiveness. He is ever disposed to show mercy.

Divine Guidance

After describing the disobedience of Adam (pbuh), the Honored Quran introduces another divine intervention that deserves a deeper consideration:

Al-Baqarah 2:37

[37] Then Adam received words from his Lord. He (his Lord) turned to him. He is ever disposed to be compassionate and merciful.

"Words from his Lord": many wonder what they are. The answer becomes quite clear if we continue reading Al-Baqarah 2:38, 39:

[38] We said: "Go forth, all of you! (but) when guidance comes to you, whoever follows it will have no fear, nor shall he grieve.

[39] And (as to) those who disbelieve in and reject My communications, they are the inmates of the fire. In it, they shall abide."

In Ayah 38, Allah promised to take away "grief" and "fear" from Adam and Eva (pbut), provided they accepted His mercy and the instruction He gives. By answering so, Allah opened a Right Way that our first parents needed to follow if they wanted to enter Paradise someday:

Ṭā Hā 20:122, 123

[122] His Lord chose him, turned to him in forgiveness and guided him.

[123] (Allah) said, "Go forth, all of you! Some of you will be enemies to one another. (but) when guidance comes to you, whoever follows it will not go astray nor suffer."

The term "guidance"—we could say "a guide"—presupposes the existence of a way out from errancy and suffering. Since Allah has provided it, accepting it means following the way. That is what the genuine *īmān* is all about; it goes much further than just saying: "O yes, I believe in Allah, His angels, His prophets, His books, the Judgment Day"; *īmān* is an attitude of unconditional trust in Allah's guidance along the Right Way.

Suppose you are a blind man on a narrow mountain path. A guide is with you. You rely on his to see what you don't see. You trust he wants the best for you: to reach the goal without stumbling. In the same way, you and I are spiritually short-sighted. We are unable to find the Way, and it is why Surah Al-Fātiḥah (the first chapter of the Honored Quran) is a cry for Allah to guide us into the Right Way.

But you will remember from Chapter 2 that "guidance" refers to the Honored Taurat, Zabur, and Injil. Could they answer our prayer for divine instruction?

Al-Mā'idah 5:46

> 46 We have sent Isa Ibn Maryam in their footsteps, confirming what was in his hands from the Taurat. We gave him the Injil, guidance, and light, confirming what was in his hands from the Taurat, a guidance and an admonition to the God-conscious.

Al-Aḥqāf 46:30

> 30 They said, "O our people! We have heard a Book sent down after Musa, confirming what came before it. It guides us into the Truth and the Right Way."

Some Verses from the Honored Bible

Related to Chapter 3

The Sacrifice of Ibrahim's (pbuh) Son

Taurat, Genesis 22:2-13 [20]

2 God said, "Take your son, your only son, whom you love—Isaac —and go to the land of Moriah. There you will sacrifice him as a burnt offering on a mountain I will indicate to you."

3 Early the next day, Ibrahim got up and loaded his donkey. He took with him two of his servants and his son Isaac. When he had cut enough wood for the burnt offering, he set out for the place God had indicated.

4 On the third day, Ibrahim looked up and saw the place in the distance.

5 He said to his servants, "Stay here with the donkey while the boy and I go over there. We will bow down and come back to you."

6 Ibrahim took the wood for the burnt offering and placed it on his son Isaac, who carried the fire and the knife. As the two advanced together,

7 Isaac spoke up and said to his father, "Father?" "Yes, my son." "The fire and the wood are there, but where is the lamb for the offering?"

8 Ibrahim replied, "My son, God will provide the lamb for the burnt offering." And they both set out.

20 Some may be surprised (or even offended) that the Honored Taurat does not name which son, but instead what the substitute provided by Allah is. I decided not to engage in this discussion because the focus of the narrative is not the identity of the son, but the meaning of the victim provided by Allah.

[9] When they reached the place God had told him about, Ibrahim built an altar and laid the wood on it. He bound his son Isaac and laid him on the altar above the wood.

[10] Then he stretched out his hand and took the knife to kill his son.

[11] But the angel of the Lord called out to him from heaven, "Ibrahim!"

He replied, "Here I am."

[12] He said, "Do not lay a hand on the boy. Do not do anything to him. I know now that you fear God because you did not refuse me your son, your only son."

[13] Ibrahim saw a ram caught by the horns in a thicket. He went over, took the ram, and sacrificed it as a burnt offering in place of his son.

The Fall of Adam and Eve (pbut)

Taurat, Genesis 3:1-9

[1] The snake was craftier than any animal the Lord God had created. He asked the woman, "Did God really forbid you to eat from all of the trees in the garden? "

[2] The woman said to the snake, "We can eat from the trees in the garden,

[3] But God told us not to eat fruit from the tree in the middle of the garden and not to touch it. Otherwise, we will die."

[4] "You will certainly not die," the snake said to the woman.

[5] "But God knows that when you eat of it, your eyes will be opened and you will be like God, knowing good and evil."

[6] The woman saw that the fruit of the tree was good to eat, pleasing to the sight, and that it gave wisdom, she took it and ate. She also gave some to her husband, who was with her, and he ate.

[7] Their eyes were opened and they realized they were naked. So they sewed fig leaves covered themselves.

8 And the man and his wife heard the sound of the Lord God walking in the garden in the cool of the day, and they hid from the Lord God among the trees of the garden.

9 But the Lord God called to the man, “Where are you?” (…)

The Cloth of Righteousness

Taurat, Genesis 3:21

21 The Lord God made garments of skin for Adam and his wife and clothed them.

Taurat, Isaiah 64:6

6 We have all become like one who is unclean, and all our acts of righteousness are like filthy rags. We all wither like a leaf, and our sins carry us away like in the wind.

Taurat, Isaiah 61:10

10 I delight in the Lord, my soul rejoices in my God because he has clothed me with a garment of salvation and arrayed me with a robe of his righteousness, as a bridegroom adorns his head after the manner of a priest, and as a bride adorns herself with her jewels.

بسم الله الرحمن الرحيم

Chapter 4

Allah Will Give Peace

As-salāmᵘ ʻalaykum, brothers and sisters! Peace be with you! Can I wish you anything more desirable than peace? Harmony in the family, good neighborliness, viable agreements between nations—yes, this is my wish for you!

As we look at Planet Earth's global situation, there are serious reasons to worry. We all long for Paradise, and as believers in the day of judgment, we know that a durable solution can only come through Allah's intervention.[21]

Beyond the hope of a world without war and injustice, Allah wants to give us *inner peace*; a clear conscience, coherence between goodwill and achievements, and—first and foremost—peace with Allah.

As soon as Shaytan led Adam and Eva [(pbut)] into disobedience, harmony got lost. A contagious disease called "evil" brought the slavery of pride, greed, vice, destructive habits, hatred, and abuse of power.

The result of moral failures is severe enough to terrify those who believe in Allah's judgment, and some stubborn habits make us cry for deliverance.

We may sometimes feel like someone who, in ancient history, falls into a debt spiral and looks for a way to escape it. But maybe a relative or a friend can show benevolence by solving his indebtedness.

Welfare organizations apply the same principle today when they give money to send mistreated animals or captive endangered species back to their natural environments. Young men can avoid compulsory military service in many countries by paying compensation. In other countries prisoners can pay for their release. Several governments are ready to pay huge sums to set kidnapped hostages free, and insurers give modern sea pirates enough cash to obtain the release of captured vessels.

---

21 I have written a book about the last days in the Honored Bible, the Honored Quran, and the Hadiths called *Longing for Paradise*. For more information, please contact me at info@hopetoshare.org.

Who Will Set Us Free?

Destructive practices create bad habits, and immorality becomes a kind of slavery. The issue we need to raise is, who will set us free? Who can pay the price for our release?

Considering our moral state and Allah's purity makes us realize that all our good deeds will never be enough to redeem us from the consequences of human insufficiency.

Humankind ultimately cannot save itself. No one can change his or her own heart. It is not enough to be told to be good. If it is our duty us to cleanse ourselves before coming to Allah, I am afraid there is no hope, for no human can make himself pure. Unpleasant thoughts come into our hearts uninvited; feelings of hatred or resentment surround us like brackish water bubbling out of an undrinkable spring. We constantly try to remove the spots, but the fountain of our heart generates toxic thoughts.

Therefore, it needs to be cleaned, but how does this work? All promises to be "good" are worthless, for humans are notorious for failing to keep their commitments. There is no way out of the moral debt trap into which all have fallen. No one is good enough to impress Allah, the righteous Judge. No one can repair the broken relationship between the perfect God and His rebellious creatures. No one can afford the high price of His justification. There is no way for us to pay for our wrongdoing, as the Honored Quran stipulates:

Az-Zumar 39:47

> 47 Even if the wrongdoers possessed all the earth's wealth and much more, they would be ready to offer it all as ransom to escape the punishment on the Day of Resurrection. However, something will appear before them that they did not anticipate.

The message is that no wrongdoer can a price high enough to get to Paradise. Nothing is sufficient to redeem them from eternal punishment. Let us first notice the use of the Arabic word for "ransom": *fidā*. It is the same root found in Surah Aṣ-Ṣāffāt to express the act of redemption as compensation in Aṣ-Ṣāffāt 37:107:

> 107 We ransomed him with a tremendous sacrifice.[22]

---

22 *Wafadaynāhu bidhib'ḥin 'aẓīmin.*

Who Paid the Ransom?

The concept of *fidyah* (in spoken Arabic, the possibility of a religious donation to redeem oneself, or the gift of self to save someone's life) has given birth to various expressions such as:

- "If only I could be your ransom!", meaning: "I wish I could give myself in your place" or "I wish I could save you even if it cost my life!" This exclamation comforts someone who has lost money or broken a treasured object[23].
- "If only I could give my life to save you!", which is what you say when you visit a sick friend or relative.[24]
- "He sacrificed his life for his home country," which is used to honor a soldier who died on the battlefield.[25]
- "He gave everything for that cause," i.e., "He gave up everything to reach his goal." Such is the comment given about a soccer player who gave his best throughout a game or a scientist who spent sweat and blood for the sake of a discovery.[26]

All these idioms suggest an exchange, a substitution for one's life, and the readiness to give everything, even one's life, to save a loved one or a country. Therefore, the mention of *fidā* in the Honored Quran implies that Allah offered a way to redeem Ibrahim's son (pbuh). In a poem ascribed to 'Umayya Ibn Abī Aṣ-Ṣalt,[27] Allah showed the animal to Ibrahim (pbuh) and told Him: "Take this *fidā* for your son!" (quoted by Ath-Tha'labī in Firestone 1990, p. 127).

As for Ibrahim's son (pbuh) Allah gave a high-value present so the son could live. That act is called *fidā*, redemption.

"Allah gave a high-value present so the son could live. That act is called *fidā*, redemption."

What about us? After affirming the impossibility of our reimbursing Allah for the price for our transgressions, the ayah I quoted previously continues with an unexpected affirmation:

---

23 *Fidāk ja'altu*!

24 *Birrūḥ afdi*!

25 *Fidā'an lilwatan mata.*

26 *Kull shay fidā' ja'ala.*

27 A poet of the Ḥanīf community who lived at the time of Muhammad (pbuh) in Arabia and who died in 631 or 632 AD /10-11 Hijrah.

Az-Zumar 39:47

47 Even if the wrongdoers possessed all the earth's wealth and much more, they would be ready to offer it all as ransom to escape the punishment on the Day of Resurrection. However, something will appear before them that they did not anticipate.

"Something will appear before them that they did not anticipate." Allow me to try a more accurate translation: Something initiated by Allah will appear to them that they had not taken into account. The Arabic *ḥisbāb* (account) is used to name the judgment day: Yawm-ul-ḥisābi, the day on which Allah will count our good and bad deeds. In other words, while "all the wealth of the earth" will not be sufficient to fulfill our debt to Allah, He will provide something to settle our "heavenly account."

Will Allah Forgive?

How good it is to know that Allah is the Merciful One! Numerous ayat of the Honored Quran underline the divine willingness to forgive:

Al-Īsra' 17:57

57 Those to whom they cry seek a way of approaching their Lord, which of them shall be the nearest; they hope for His mercy and fear His doom. Your Lord's doom is to be shunned.

Ash-Shu'arā' 26:80-82

80 When I sicken, then He heals me.
81 And who causes me to die, then gives me life again.
82 And who, I ardently hope, will acquit me of my sins on the Day of Judgment.

An-Nasr 110:3

3 Celebrate the praise of your Lord and seek His forgiveness. He is ever disposed to show mercy.

Even more impressive is to discover *by what means* Allah made our acquittal concrete, for such an act cannot be accomplished without a price to be paid. The dilemma is, how can Allah be compassionate and righteous at the same time? He is merciful, but His righteousness cannot let injustice go unpunished. The following story helps us grasp the concept of redemption.

One of the first things I do when going abroad is to buy a local SIM card. Recently, while waiting at the counter, I heard a cry: "A thief! Hold him!" Just before me was a young man who had just grabbed a packaged smartphone. He ran but was finally caught. Outside, I asked my driver what would happen next. He answered with one word: "Death." The crowd would pour petrol on an old tire, squeeze the thug into it, and light them both. The process would be short unless the police were able to make it through the crowd in time to prevent mob justice.

To protect my feelings from the thought of this horrible outcome, I let my imagination work out a happy ending that might have looked like the following:

The man stands in front of the judge. While accusations pour down on him, a voice from the courtroom shouts:

"Wait! This man is my neighbor. He is a good man who has stolen only in mere desperation. I know he has no job, and his family lives hand to mouth. I believe, Mr. Prosecutor, you should turn a blind eye."

Murmurs of empathy spread around the hall. Many have tears in their eyes. Isn't it a sad world we're living in? Shouldn't this man be treated with greatness of spirit?

"Hold on," the business owner says, "if you acquit that man, thousands will ransack my shop—each with a good excuse for stealing. Eventually, *I* will be the one deprived. And after all, I have suffered an injustice. I want my money back."

While the judge considers the objection, something unexpected occurs: he realizes that the thief is the son of his childhood friend. This puts him in a predicament. The tender spot in his heart urges him to spare the young man from the fine he deserves. The problem is that acquitting him would be a conflict of interest.

After further deep reflection, the judge decides to keep his verdict. But then he surprises the court by pulling his checkbook out of his pocket and paying the fine for the accused. Thus, justice is done, and the shopkeeper has no right to complain anymore.

What a feeling of release for the culprit! He is acquitted. He can breathe freely and does not need to pay a cent. He who could have suffered a gruesome death leaves the courthouse as if he had never stolen, and he feels deep relief. He is grateful for the rest of his days. Indeed, how much compassion did the judge demonstrate? He who was not guilty and did not need to pay a cent paid the fine.

A Cry for Mercy

Granted, such a story does not occur very often, but it illustrates the concept of redemption well. When Adam and Eva (pbut) rebelled against Allah, He, the mighty God of the universe, could have quickly annihilated them:

'Āli 'Imrān 3:26

> 26 O Lord, Owner of Sovereignty! You bestow sovereignty on whom You will and take it from whom You will; You exalt and dishonor whom You will. In Your hands lies all that is good; You have power over all things.

Adam and Eva (pbut) repented of their mistake and longed for forgiveness. That is why they eventually prayed:

Al-A'rāf 7:23

> 23 They said, "Our Lord! We have cheated ourselves. And if you do not grant pardon and do not have no mercy on us, we will surely be lost!"

The dilemma is, how should Allah forgive? Can the Holy One revoke His verdict? No way! And neither can humankind modify Allah's Words! The decision is irrevocable: Allah's justice demands a just punishment.

Adam and Eva (pbut) misused Allah's goodness. Even though they repented, one wonders if this was enough to repair such a broken relationship. We all know by experience how difficult it is to forget an offense. No matter what you give or do to make it good, it creates the feeling of not being sufficient.

Surprisingly, Allah did not destroy Adam and Eva (pbut), and He did not annihilate humanity. Allah is full of goodwill toward us. Like a loving father, the One who created us from dust pities us. Because He cares for us, He wants to save us. Like the judge who paid instead of the thief, Allah took the initiative and imparted His compassion through an action that has amazed the prophets and messengers (pbut) throughout the centuries:

Al-A'rāf 7:72

> 72 We saved him and those who adhered to him by our mercy, and We cut off the roots of those who rejected our Signs and did not believe.

The immediate context shows that the above ayah does not directly apply to Adam and Eva (pbut). Yet it is in the same surah and may be taken as an answer to the cry of Adam and Eva (pbut) and many others for relief:

Nuh (pbuh) (Hūd 11:47):

> 47 “My Lord, I seek refuge with You while asking You something I do not know. And if You do not forgive me and have mercy on me, I shall certainly be lost.”

Musa and his brother Aaron/Harun (pbut) (Al-A‘rāf 7:151):

> 151 “My Lord, have mercy on me and my brother. Bring us into Your mercy; You are the Merciful and compassionate.”

Yusuf (pbuh) (Yūsuf 12:53):

> 53 “I do not ever free myself of blame; the human soul is certainly prone to iniquity unless my Lord bestows His mercy; indeed, my Lord is Forgiving and merciful.”

Muhammad (pbuh) (Al-Mu’minūn 23:118):

> 118 “My Lord! Grant pardon and have mercy, for You are the best of the relenting!”

Could it be that such a desperate appeal for forgiveness is also *yours and mine*? You and I long for compassion, and Allah’s *raḥmat* is the answer because it is the answer to the problem of shame and guilt. It is the healing cure for our fear of Allah. *Allah wants to make peace with and within you.* He wants to give you perfect peace of mind. That is divine medicine!

Al-An‘ām 6:12

> 12 “To whom belongs whatever is in the heavens and earth?” Say, “To Allah.” He has decreed upon Himself mercy and will assemble you for the Resurrection Day, about which there is no doubt. Whoever does not believe will be lost.

Allah has revealed that humanity can only escape condemnation by trusting in His mercy. Allah is the One who can grant pardon, and no one else can show the way to salvation. Allah “has written mercy on His soul,” and because of that, He will assemble us for the Resurrection Day. What a comforting thought!

The Right Way

As we have read in the Honored Quran, Allah promised to guide Adam and Eva (pbut). The text continues by offering the good news of a way out for all those who want to "stop grieving": Allah's promises to remove our "grief" and "fear." This is the way to Paradise:

Al-Baqarah 2:38

> 38 We said: "Go forth, all of you! (but) when guidance comes to you, whoever follows it will have no fear, nor shall he grieve."

Ṭā Hā 20:122, 123

> 122 His Lord chose him, turned to him in forgiveness and guided him.
> 123 (Allah) said, "Go forth, all of you! Some of you will be enemies to one another. (but) when guidance comes to you, whoever follows it will not go astray nor suffer."

Thus, the Honored Quran answers the prayer for guidance in the Right Way. The way is to "follow him":

'Āli 'Imrān 3:31

> 31 If you love Allah, follow me! Allah will love you and erase your wrongdoings. Allah is the Forgiving, the Merciful.

I invite you to rejoice in anticipating eternity in Paradise. May you make the same decision as Ibrahim, Allah's friend (pbuh), and turn in His footsteps! May your heart become like a refreshing oasis in the desert! May the water of life coming from Allah revive the world with happiness and peace!

Az-Zumar 39:53

> 53 Say, "O My servants who have transgressed against themselves, do not doubt the mercy of Allah. Indeed, Allah forgives all sins. Indeed, He is the Forgiver, the Merciful."

Some Verses from the Honored Bible

Related to Chapter 4

Not a Single Act of Goodness Can Bring Us Closer to Allah

Taurat, Micah 6:6, 7

6 With what shall I present myself before the Lord and bow down before the Most High? Shall I come before Him with burnt offerings, with calves a year old?
7 Will the Lord be pleased with thousands of rams and ten thousand rivers of olive oil? Shall I offer my firstborn for my wickedness, the fruit of my body for the sin of my soul?

Injil, Epistle of Paul to the Ephesians 2:8, 9

8 For it is by grace you have been saved, through faith.
It is not of yourselves; it is God's gift.
9 Not by works, so that no one can boast.

Taqwāh and the "Lamb Coming from Allah"

Taurat, Isaiah 53:4-7

4 Surely, he took up our pain and carried our sorrows. However, we considered him punished, stricken, and afflicted by God.
5 But he was pierced for our transgressions and crushed for our iniquities; the punishment that brought us peace was upon him, and by his wounds we are healed.
6 We all went astray like sheep. We have turned aside from our way, and the Lord has laid on him all our iniquity.
7 He was oppressed and mistreated, yet he did not open his mouth. He was led like a lamb to the slaughter, and, like a sheep silent before its shearers, he did not open his mouth.

Injil, 1st Epistle of Peter 1:18-20

18 You know that you were not redeemed by perishable things, such as silver or gold, from the empty way of life handed down to you from your ancestors,

19 but by the precious blood of Christ, a lamb without blemish and without spot.

20 He was chosen before the creation of the world, but he has been revealed in these last times, for your sake.

بسم الله الرحمن الرحيم

Chapter 5

Does Allah Have a Son? The Truth About Al-Masih Isa ibn Maryam (piuh)

The Honored Quran does well when it states that Al-Masih Isa ibn Maryam (piuh) is *not* the physical *child* of Allah. All Muslims are familiar with the words of Surah Al-Ikhlāṣ 112:1-4:

1 Say: "He is Allah, the One!
2 Allah, the Eternal!
3 He does not beget nor was begotten.
4 And there is none comparable unto Him."

"Allah is One." Indeed, the doctrine of *tawḥīd*, the oneness of Allah, is so fundamental that it is placed at the beginning of the *Shahāda*. *Lā 'ilāh*[a] *ilā Allah*: "There is no other God beside Allah!" Indeed, there is no worse blasphemy than to ascribe an associate to Him:

An-Nisā' 4:116

116 Allah will not forgive whenever partners are ascribed to Him. He pardons all except those to whom He will. Whoever ascribes partners to Allah has wandered far astray.

The same surah exposes the distorted conception of Allah that some of the People of the Book used to have:

An-Nisā' 4:171

> 171 People of the Book! Do not deviate from your religion and only tell the truth about Allah. Al-Masih Isa ibn Maryam is truly Allah's messenger, His word conveyed to Maryam and spirit from Him. Therefore, believe in Allah and His messengers, and do not say "Three!" Abstain! (It will be) better for you! Allah is only (truly) One God. Glory to Him! Far is it removed from His transcendent majesty that He should have a child! To Him belong whatever is in the heavens and all that is in the earth. And Allah is sufficient as a Defender.

A brief look at church history confirms that some Christians who lived in the time of Muhammad (pbuh) had confused the truth about Jesus (piuh) with pagan thoughts: Some believed that Allah had taken a wife and made her part of the Godhead and that Jesus (piuh) was born from that "divine alliance" as the physical child of Allah. Some others alleged that Allah had adopted a human (Jesus (piuh)) to make a God out of him, and called him "His son." A specific group considered Maryam the third person of what most Christians call "the Trinity." Others called Maryam "Allah's mother." May Allah forbid such blasphemous thoughts! These derived from Greek paganism, and some tried to introduce them into the Christian faith. The Honored Quran proscribes the teaching of this specific group of believers.

Surah Al-Mā'idah 5:82, for instance, reprehends the *mush'rikūn*—generally translated as "idolaters" or "polytheists" and applied to pagans and some Christian groups (the Adoptionists). The *mush'rikūn* were Christians who taught that Jesus (piuh) was a man who reached perfection and got rewarded for it by becoming an "associate" to God; in other words, they said that God adopted Jesus (piuh) as His "son" while he was baptized and conferred divinity to him. This is one point the Honored Quran refutes, vehemently rebuking those who associate any partner with Allah.

However, it is essential to know that no Christian endorses such teachings anymore, and that is why the Honored Quran does not consider Christians to be polytheists.

Yet the Honored Quran makes a distinction between them and the *naṣārā*, generally understood as "Christians." That might be a reference to the two groups of followers of Jesus (piuh) which I identified in the first chapter of this book.

Another Christian heresy, Modalism, teaches that the oneness of Allah does not consist in three simultaneous persons but in three intermittent apparitions of the same and unique God. Consequently, complete godliness was in Isa (piuh) while he was on Earth. In answer, the Quran denies that Allah is (only) Isa (piuh). Almost all Christians today refute Modalism.

Al-Mā'idah 5:72

> 72 They indeed hide something, those who say that Allah is Al-Masih Isa ibn Maryam, while Al-Masih (himself) said: "O children of Israel, worship Allah, my Lord, and your Lord." Whoever ascribes partners to Allah, for him Allah has forbidden paradise: his abode is the Fire. For wrongdoers, there will be no helper.

Al-An'ām 6:101

> 101 Initiator of heaven and earth, how can He have a child? He has no spouse! He has created everything and is aware of everything.

Since the doctrine of Adoptionism has disappeared in the course of history, the sin of *shirk* (association) does not apply to Christianity today. Yet, one may ask whether Christians have several gods. Does the formula "There is no God beside Allah" contradict the Honored Injil? The answer is in the quranic affirmation that all descendants of Ibrahim (pbuh) have the same God. The most explicit text in that regard is Surah Al-'Ankabūt 29:46:

> 46 If you argue with the People of the Book, do it only in the most courteous way—except with those who do wrong; and say: "We believe in what has been sent down to you and us. Our God and your God is one, and we submit to Him."

The Oneness of the Christian God

While the doctrine of the oneness of Allah is fundamental to Islam, I do not think it contradicts Judaism or Christianity—on the contrary! Two thousand years before Muhammad (pbuh), Musa (pbuh) taught his people the Jewish equivalent of the Muslim *Shahāda*:

"Two thousand years before Muhammad (pbuh), Musa (pbuh) taught his people the Jewish equivalent of the Muslim *Shahāda*:"

Taurat, Deuteronomy 6:4

> 4 Listen, Israel! The Lord our God, the Lord is One.

The first part of the *Shahāda* appears several times in the Honored Taurat; like, for example, in Taurat, Isaiah 45:5a:

[5a] I am the Lord, and there is no god besides Me.

Moreover, Jesus (piuh) himself quoted the *tawḥīd* in connection with the "most important commandment":

Injil, Gospel of Mark 12:28-32

[28] One day, a theologian pushed Jesus into a debate, asking him: "Which commandment is the most important?"
[29] "The most important," Jesus replied, "is this: 'Listen, Israel! The Lord our God, the Lord is one.
[30] Love the Lord your God with all your heart, with all your soul, with all your mind, and with all your strength.'
[31] The second (commandment) is this: 'Love your neighbor as yourself.' There is no greater commandment than these."
[32] "Well said, teacher," the man replied, "You are right to say that God is one and that there is no other but him."

Notice that the Honored Injil confirms the principle of Allah's oneness, quoting the Jewish *Shahāda* with the exact words found in the Muslim *Shahāda*!

The Meaning of "Son of God"

To the deep discontentment of most Muslims, the Honored Injil calls Jesus (piuh) "Son of man" and sometimes "Son of God." As soon as Muslims and Christians come to this point of discussion, they think they have reached an insurmountable wall. However, we must ask what this affirmation means:

- Does it imply that Jesus (piuh) is to be considered God's *physical* child?
- Do Christians mean by this that their God has a wife and carnal desires?

Every Christian would immediately reply, "No! By no means!" Even though every Muslim (and every Christian) believes that God/Allah created him, none would presume to title himself "*the* son of God"! On the other hand, we should not read something in the Honored Quran that is not there. The Honored Quran *never* states that:

- Allah has *no* "son" (*ibn*),
- Al-Masih Isa ibn Maryam (piuh) is *not* the son of Allah.

Instead, the Honored Quran states that:

- Allah has no physical "child" (*walad*). See An-Nisā' 4:171: "Far is it removed from His transcendent majesty that He should have a child."
- Allah cannot have a physical child since He is not a human being to be married. That is why Surah Al-An'ām 6:101 expresses some incomprehension: "Initiator of heaven and earth, how can He have a child? He has no spouse! He has created everything and is aware of everything."
- Therefore, Al-Masih Isa ibn Maryam (piuh) is not "son of God" as a result of a physical union in which Allah was involved.

If this is all the case, we need to search for another explanation for the concept of "son of God." The answer is that we are not dealing with a *theological* issue but with some *linguistic* confusion; in other words, we face a *misunderstanding* between Christianity and Islam rather than a *contradiction.* Let me explain this to you:

There is a difference between "child" and "son." In an oriental mindset, the word "son" can be used in a literal or a figurative sense. In Arabic countries, Turkey, and the surrounding cultures, a mother may well call her naughty child *ibn Shaytān* (son of Satan). Does that mean that her son is the biological result of a relationship with Satan? Of course not! It just means that the child is behaving like a little devil! Egyptians are often called the "sons of the Nile." Is that supposed to mean that a river called the Nile has begotten them? Of course not! Again, this title must be understood as a metaphor! The same principle applies to the expression *ibn-as-sabil* (son of the road) in Surah Al-Baqarah 2:177 (still used in many oriental cultures to welcome a guest from afar).

Al-Masih Isa ibn Maryam (piuh) was born and raised in Palestine. That is also where he grew up, healed, and taught. There, too, the word "son" was used figuratively. That is why the word "son" is often mentioned in the Honored Bible but not in a physical sense. Several texts confirm this interpretation. In the Taurat, Allah calls the people of Israel: "my sons" and refers to Solomon (pbuh) as his "son":

Taurat, Hosea 11:1

> 1 When Israel was a child, I loved him and called my son out of Egypt.

Taurat, 2nd Samuel 7:14

> 14 I will be his Father, and he will be my son.

In the Honored Injil, the Apostle Paul rebukes a magician by treating him as a "son of the Devil."

Injil, Acts of the Apostles 13:10

> [10] You, son of the devil and enemy of justice. Will you never cease to pervert the upright ways of the Lord?

One day Jesus (piuh) told some Jews, "You are the children of your father the Devil," and then he added, "He is a liar, and the father of all lies."

Injil, Gospel of John 8:39, 42, 44:

> [39] They answered, "Abraham is our father." Jesus told them, "If you were Abraham's children, you would do Abraham's works!
> [42] If God was your Father, you would love me, for I came from God; nor did I come of myself, but he sent me.
> [44] You are of your father the Devil, and you want to fulfill your father's desires. He is a murderer from the beginning and does not stand in the truth because there is no truth in him. When he speaks lies, he speaks from his resources because he is a liar and the father of lies."

The word "son" is used in Semitic cultures as an illustration to express mainly two characteristics:

- In a figurative sense, a "son" is someone who is similar to, or acts in the same way as, a "father" (see expressions like "Son of Satan").
- A "son" is a representative, an ambassador authorized to act on behalf of his country, a businessman who negotiates in the name of a company, or a (physical) son commissioned by his father.

Since the Honored Taurat, Zabur, Injil, and Quran all use the word "son" as a metaphor, we have no choice but to interpret the expression "Jesus, son of God" (piuh) in a symbolic way. Does it mean that Jesus (piuh) is *not* the literal son (child) of Allah as the product of a physical union? Yes, that is true.

Moreover, Al-Masih (piuh) is called "Ibn Maryam" (son of a woman), which opens the debate about his father. Maybe we do not know who he was because Maryam was a woman with a bad life. May Allah forbid such a thought!

Christians and Muslims share the common belief in the supernatural birth of Al-Masih Isa ibn Maryam (piuh). All their holy books affirm that a Spirit of divine origin entered Maryam. This is why Christians call him the "son of Allah." The Honored Quran describes him with several peculiarities that show his supernatural nature. Therefore, both religions are not very far from each other on that point, except for the problem of understanding the expression of "Son of Allah." Let us list the features that the Honored Quran confers to Al-Masih Isa ibn Maryam (piuh).

Ibn Maryam (The Son of Mary[28])

In no less than twenty-five ayat, Al-Masih Isa (piuh) is named "Ibn Maryam." Orientals would typically say: "Son of Ali" or "Son of Abd al-Fattah," i.e., son of a father named Ali or Abd al-Fattah. We all know famous theologians such as Isma'il *Ibn* Kathir (Ishmael, son of Kathir), Ali *Ibn* Muhammad, Abd al-Faraj *Ibn* al-Jauzi or Abd ar-Rahman *Ibn* 'Ali.

However, no one would ever use the mother's name instead of the father's. There is one exception: Ibn Maryam (piuh). What may be the cause for it? The answer is that Al-Masih Isa (piuh) never had a physical father, and that is why he is called "Ibn Maryam" (son of … a woman)!

Why, then, is Jesus (piuh) called the "Son of Allah"? It is because Allah has sent him with a unique message. It explains why he is also called *rasūl Ullah* (Allah's messenger).

Rasūl Ullah (Allah's Messenger)

The word *rasūl* occurs 332 times in the Honored Quran, and, needless to say, there are many other "messengers" besides Al-Masih Isa ibn Maryam (piuh). Even if several are named *rasūl Allah*, "Allah's messenger," the question is whether some messengers are privileged. If so, which ones have a specific status? Whatever you think, your answer must be taken from the Honored Quran. The following ayah deals with our issue:

Al-Baqarah 2:253

> 253 We have privileged some of those Messengers. Allah spoke directly to some, while He raised others to a high position. But We gave Isa ibn Maryam clear signs and supported him through the Holy Spirit.

---

28 Most Christians call her "Mary." As a bridge to Muslims, it is interesting to note that the Honored Injil sometimes names her "Mary" (Greek *María*) and sometimes "Maryam" (*Maryám*). The Hebrew word is *Miriam*.

This ayah makes a clear distinction between the messengers. While there is no doubt that all of them are important, some "have been privileged," and others "raised to a high position."

Please note that only one messenger is mentioned here by name: Al-Masih Isa ibn Maryam (piuh). Is it pure coincidence, or does the text point to a specific message to be discovered? Does the Honored Quran reveal more about some unique attention given to Al-Masih Isa ibn Maryam (piuh)?

Let us answer by looking at all twenty-five quranic texts about Al-Masih Isa ibn Maryam (piuh) individually.

Rūḥ min-hu (Spirit Coming from Him)

Al-Masih Isa ibn Maryam (piuh) is the only one in the whole Honored Quran who was supported through Allah's Spirit:

Al-Mā'idah 5:110a

> 110a Allah said: "O Isa ibn Maryam, remember My favor to you and your mother when I strengthened you with the Holy Spirit...."

The Arabic word *ayyada* (to support), does not specify the kind of "support" Allah gave Al-Masih (piuh). Two other ayat, though, give an explanation: Al-Masih Isa ibn Maryam (piuh) was sent into this world through Allah's Spirit breathed into Maryam:

Al-Anbiyā' 21:91

> 91 We (Allah) breathed from Our Spirit into (the woman) who guarded her chastity, and We made her and her son a sign for the worlds.

At-Taḥrīm 66:12

> 12 Allah has given Maryam, 'Imran's daughter, as an example. She preserved her purity, and We breathed of Our Spirit into her womb. She put her trust in the words of her Lord and His Scriptures and was genuinely devout.

Al-Masih Isa ibn Maryam (piuh) was born through Allah's Spirit breathed into his mother. There is much more to discover. He is also the only prophet/messenger called "Spirit coming from Allah":

An-Nisā' 4:171b

> 171b Al-Masih Isa ibn Maryam is truly Allah's messenger, His Word conveyed to Maryam and spirit from Him.

Al-Masih (The Messiah)

The most relevant ayah about Al-Masih Isa ibn Maryam (piuh) is probably 'Āli 'Imrān 3:45. Let us read it:

> 45 When the angels said, "O, Maryam! Allah gives the good news of a Word from Him, whose name is Al-Masih Isa ibn Maryam. He is glorious in this world and the next, one of those who are near to Allah."

Most people think that the name Al-Masih has no special meaning. Maybe it is just a nickname or a family name, as people commonly have in Western countries. But epithets, especially in an oriental mindset, have a precise meaning; they are supposed to reflect the character of their bearer.

Moreover, we read that Allah said to Maryam: "His name is …" which means that his appellation was not given by any parents or relatives but by Allah Himself. That is why he is called *Al-Masih*: the Messiah. According to the Honored Quran, Al-Masih Isa ibn Maryam (piuh) is the only one who carries the title Al-Masīḥ. *Masīḥ* stems from the Arabic verb *masaḥa*, meaning: "to stroke, to rub" or, in a unique sense, when in connection with oil: "to anoint"[29] (Cowan 1979, p. 907). Several Arabic nouns show how this word root was applied.[30] The title "Al-Masih" comes from the Honored Taurat, used when kings were anointed with special oil. "Anointed" means "chosen." Al-Masih Isa ibn Maryam (piuh) is truly Allah's Chosen one!

Al-Masih (piuh) Purifies and Heals

The verb *masaḥa* has a second meaning: "to wipe off/out/away; to wash; to clean; to erase; to take away." It is also used to signify applying olive oil to a wound to heal it. Thus, Al-Masih is the one who purifies and heals.

During his Egyptian campaign, the French Emperor Napoleon heard *masaḥa* and created the French noun *massage*. Therefore, we can compare Al-Masih Isa ibn Maryam (piuh) with a physiotherapist.

- *Al-Masih relaxes us when we are laden with sorrow.*
- *Al-Masih shields us from harmful influences*; like oil does, which protects our skin from sunburn.
- We rub on some cream to hide a scar. Indeed, *Al-Masih cures us from emotional injuries.*

29 Also "to take away, to withdraw."

30 *Masḥa*: rubbing, embrocation; *masḥ*: a land surveyor (searching a map by moving one's hand over it); *misāḥa*: a surface, etc.

- Scrubbing cleans away the skin's impurities. In the same way, *Al-Masih purifies us from the moral spot.*
- The purpose of makeup is to make us look good, and *Al-Masih truly makes our faces shine.*
- Physiotherapy provides wellness to both body and soul, and *Al-Masih gives peace of mind and genuine happiness.*
- *Al-Masih, therefore, is the one who gives us wellness in the sense of the word salām*: inner peace.

Because Al-Masih Isa ibn Maryam (piuh) is the one who purifies and heals, the Honored Quran invites us to put our confidence in him, just like you would fully submit to a chiropractor giving you a manipulation.

> "The Honored Quran invites us to put our confidence in Al-Masih Isa ibn Maryam (piuh)."

Isa (Jesus (piuh))

What about *Isa*, the second part of his name? Does it have a specific meaning? Not in Arabic, but yes in Hebrew, in which *Yeshua* originally means "the one who intervenes at the last moment when the situation looks desperate" (Gesenius 1962, p. 324);[31] for example, one who reaches down into a deep well and pulls out whoever cannot get out by himself.

Therefore, *Isa* refers to someone who offers a tangible solution to our needs and problems. The fact that this name was given to Maryam by the angels on behalf of Allah suggests that its meaning is not a coincidence. As we will see later, Al-Masih Isa ibn Maryam (piuh) can heal, resurrect the dead, and do many other miracles.

Kalimat Ullah (Allah's Word)

Furthermore, let us remark that no other besides Al-Masih Isa ibn Maryam (piuh) is named "a word from Him." In An-Nisā' 4:171, he is even called "His Word":

> [171b] Al-Masih Isa ibn Maryam is truly Allah's messenger, His Word conveyed to Maryam and spirit from Him.

31 *'Isā* stems from *Iēsus*, the Greek form of the Hebrew name *Yeshua*.

The way someone speaks reveals who she or he is and what she or he thinks. As long as someone keeps silent, she or he remains mysterious even if we look at their outward appearance. Thus, the "word" is the disclosure or, we may say, the revelation (the unveiling) of someone's character. Whoever has nothing to hide will speak clearly so that we can know what she or he means.

Suppose for a moment that an attractive person has stolen your heart. Then he or she begins to speak, and what he or she says gives you a horrible sensation. Your interest in this person melts as quickly as an ice block in the sunshine.

With Allah, it is the other way around.

You may think of Him as a fearsome God. This is why He sent Al-Masih Isa ibn Maryam (piuh) in such a unique capacity: being His Word to make His thoughts audible in a language humans can understand. He wanted to communicate with us and show us who He is.

That is why He reached out to us through His Word. Whoever listens to this word immediately feels attracted by His wondrous love.

Wajīh wa muqarrab (Glorious and Near to Allah)

Al-Masih Isa ibn Maryam (piuh) is the only one "glorious in this world and the next." The statement confirms the exceptional status of Al-Masih (piuh). More than that, Al-Masih Isa ibn Maryam (piuh) occupies this status in both Allah's sphere and our world. It is said that Prophet Moses/Musa (pbuh) is also exalted *in this world*, but no one else is pointed out as having such a high level in both worlds.

Moreover, Al-Masih Isa ibn Maryam (piuh) is the only one called "One who is near to Allah":

'Āli 'Imrān 3:45

> 45 When the angels said, "O, Maryam! Allah gives the good news of a Word from Him, whose name is Al-Masih Isa ibn Maryam. He is glorious in this world and the next, one of those who are near to Allah."

Angels are also said to be near to Allah. While no one can ever pretend to be physically close to Allah, the indication "near to Allah" implies a supernatural standing, and Al-Masih Isa ibn Maryam (piuh) has indeed been raised to Allah's presence in Heaven. Al-Masih Isa ibn Maryam (piuh) is alive, and right now, he is near Allah or near to Allah.

Ayāh lil-'ālamīn (A Sign for the Worlds)

Furthermore, Al-Masih Isa ibn Maryam (piuh) is the only one called "A sign from Allah." He is "a sign for mankind" (*lilnnāsi*) and "for the universe" (*lil'ālamīna*):

Maryam 19:21

> 21 He (the angel) said, "So shall it be; your Lord says, 'This is something easy for Me to make him a sign for mankind and a mercy from Us. It is a matter decreed.'"

Al-Anbiyā' 21:91

> 91 We (Allah) breathed from Our Spirit into (the woman) who guarded her chastity, and We made her and her son a sign for the worlds.

Many think that Al-Masih Isa ibn Maryam (piuh) is a sign only for Christians. But the Honored Quran says he is a sign for *all* people. Moreover, "Allah's sign" is a significant theme in the Honored Quran, designating a warning to humans. The Arabic word for "verse" (*ayāh*) means "sign." Every ayah of the Honored Quran is called a sign. Yet Al-Masih Isa ibn Maryam (piuh) did not just receive signs from Allah. He *is* a sign!

Raḥmat min-nā (A Mercy from Us)

To appreciate the importance of the word "mercy," let us take a moment to look at what happened when Adam and Eva (pbut) went the wrong way. The Honored Quran reports on Allah's reaction: He searched for them in the garden and talked to them. Then they repented of their decision, and in their longing for justification, they cried to Allah:

Al-A'rāf 7:23

> 23 They said, "Our Lord! We have cheated ourselves. And if you do not grant pardon and do not have no mercy on us, we will surely be lost!"

Allah answers the prayer of Adam, Eva (pbut), and ours. He saves through His mercy. Even though this act of compassion is not explicitly related to Adam and Eva (pbut), Allah's answer confirms that *raḥmat* (mercy) is indeed the agent of rescue. Al-A'rāf 7:71, 72 emphasizes the need to escape from His "punishment and wrath," —which is nothing other than the definition of salvation:

> [71] He said: "Punishment and wrath have already come upon you from your Lord. Do you dispute with me over names that you have devised, you and your fathers, without authority from Allah? Then wait! I am among you, also waiting."
> [72] We saved him and those with him by our mercy, and We cut off the roots of those who denied our signs and did not believe.

Here is the remedy the Honored Quran gives to everyone who fears Allah's "punishment and wrath": His mercy is the answer to the cry of Adam and Eva (pbut) and many other prophets.[32]

I must admit that such a desperate appeal for acquittal is yours and mine. You and I long for grace, and grace originating from Allah is the answer.

Allah's mercy is the answer to the problem of shame and guilt. It is the cure for our fear of Allah, the medicine that gives real peace of mind. It shows that Allah wants to be on good terms with you. Allah wants to provide you with peace in your heart—everlasting harmony. He "has written mercy on His soul";[33] because of that, "He will surely assemble us for the Resurrection Day."

Al-An'ām 6:12

> [12] "To whom belongs whatever is in the heavens and earth?" Say, "To Allah." He has decreed upon Himself mercy and will assemble you for the Resurrection Day, about which there is no doubt. Whoever does not believe will be lost.

Who Is *Raḥmat min-nā* (Mercy from Us)?

Raḥmat is not solely a divine feature. After all, several prophets (pbut) are called *Raḥmat-Ullah* (Allah's mercy) in the Honored Quran. However, when followed by the suffix *min-nā* (originating from Allah), this title refers to a specific person, the only one referred to by his name:

Al-Anbiyā' 21:107

> [107] We sent you as a mercy for the universe.

---

32 Refer to examples cited on pp. 95, 96.

33 *Kataba 'alā nafsihi l-raḥmata* (He has written mercy upon His soul)!

To whom is the above ayah referring? The superficial answer is that it is about Muhammad (pbuh). However, unlike the other prophets and messengers called by name in Surah 21 of Al-Anbiyā' (which means "The Prophets"), no name is given in connection with the godly *raḥmat*. However, the mention of *Raḥmat-Ullah* in Surah Al-Anbiyā' 21:107 may apply to Al-Masih (piuh).

The immediate context in Ayah 89 introduces Zakariya/Zachariah (pbuh) and in 90 his son Yaḥya (pbuh)—who, by the way, was the cousin of Al-Masih Isa ibn Maryam (piuh). Then in Ayah 91 Maryam the mother of Al-Masih Isa ibn Maryam (piuh) is named together with her son:

Al-Anbiyā' 21:91

> 91 We (Allah) breathed from Our Spirit into (the woman) who guarded her chastity, and We made her and her son a sign for the worlds.

The context of this statement deals with the judgment day (Ayat 92-106). Then comes Ayah 107—which I quoted a moment ago—that brings up a "mercy for the worlds." Many assume this appellation refers to the next in line, which could be Muhammad (pbuh). But suddenly, the topic switches to the family of Al-Masih Isa ibn Maryam (piuh), and the same phrase is repeated in the same surah (Anbiyā' 21:91 and 107). Both ayat use the same expression, *lil'alamina* (for the worlds), and the first one refers explicitly to Al-Masih Isa ibn Maryam (piuh).

Therefore, applying "mercy" to Al-Masih, as implied in the second ayah, seems more appropriate. This consideration is supported by the fact that the Honored Quran mentions only one person as being the "mercy from Us (Allah)," and this is Al-Masih Isa ibn Maryam (piuh)[34]:

Maryam 19:21

> 21 He (the angel) said, "So shall it be; your Lord says, 'This is something easy for Me to make him a sign for mankind and a mercy from Us. It is a matter decreed.'"

There is no doubt to whom the text applies. Al-Masih Isa ibn Maryam (piuh) is the only one introduced by name in the Honored Quran as "A mercy coming from Allah," and that is why he is the only answer to the outcry of Adam and Eva (pbut) and ultimately of every human.

---

34 *Raḥmat min-nā.*

The Good News of a Mercy

Allah's compassion is good news, and it became palpable through Al-Masih Isa ibn Maryam (piuh), as the Honored Quran declares:

At-Tawbah 9:21

> 21 Their Lord gives them good tidings of mercy from Him and approval of gardens for them with enduring pleasure.

'Āli 'Imrān 3:45

> 45 When the angels said, "O, Maryam! Allah gives the good news of a word from Him, whose name is Al-Masih Isa ibn Maryam. He is glorious in this world and the next, one of those who are near to Allah."

A word-by-word translation unveils a mind-blowing truth: Allah makes the good news real through a word from Him. It means that Al-Masih Isa ibn Maryam (piuh) is the way given by Allah to receive the Good News of divine origin. Indeed, divine kindness answers humanity's cry for redemption. The sentence "This is a matter decreed" implies that the mercy given in Al-Masih Isa ibn Maryam (piuh) was part of the divine plan prepared long before it was carried out. This explains why the Honored Quran invites us:

"A word-by-word translation unveils a mind-blowing truth: Allah makes the good news real through a word from Him."

Az-Zumar 39:53

> 53 Say, "O My servants who have transgressed against themselves, do not doubt the mercy of Allah. Indeed, Allah forgives all sins. Indeed, He is the Forgiver, the Merciful."

Az-zakī (The Pure One)

Al-Masih Isa ibn Maryam (piuh) is the only one called "The pure one":

Maryam 19:19

> 19 He (Gabriel/Jibraeel) said, "I am only a messenger of your Lord (to announce to you) the gift of a pure son."

No other human has ever been called "the pure" (*az-zakī*). No other has ever reached the incomparable character of Al-Masih Isa ibn Maryam (piuh). His life was indeed a perfect demonstration of purity.

Mubārak (Blessed)

While Muslims add to the name of every other prophet and messenger: "Peace *be* upon Him," Al-Masih Isa ibn Maryam (piuh) is the only one after whose name we say, "Peace *is* upon Him." While we ask Allah to bless all other prophets/messengers, Al-Masih Isa ibn Maryam (piuh) is the only one called "blessed." I invite you to read with me the words of Surah Maryam 19:31:

> 31 He has blessed me wherever I may be and has commanded me to pray and give alms to the poor as long as I live.

In the Honored Quran, the word "blessed" occurs only once in connection with a person, and that person is Al-Masih Isa ibn Maryam (piuh). He is the one who can pass the *barakat Ullah* (Allah's blessing) on to us.

Qaul al-Ḥaqq (The Expression of the Truth)

Maryam 19:34

> 34 Such was Isa Ibn Maryam, an expression of the truth about which they vainly dispute.

Al-Masih Isa ibn Maryam (piuh) is the only one called "the expression of the truth," whereas *ḥaqq* means truth and even more: It describes what is correct, appropriate, or necessary. *Ḥaqq* is one of Allah's ninety-nine names. Therefore, the Honored Quran presents Al-Masih (piuh) as expressing some supernatural attributes. How is that possible? As we have noted, it is because he is introduced three times with *min-Allah*, "originating from Allah":

- *raḥmat[un] min-nā*: "Mercy (coming) from Us (Allah)" in Surah Maryam 19:21
- *rūḥ[un] min-hu*: "Spirit (coming) from Him (Allah)" in An-Nisā' 4:171
- *kalimat[un] min-hu*: "Word (coming) from Him (Allah)" in 'Āli 'Imrān 3:45

This grammatical construction implies that, according to the Honored Quran, Al-Masih Isa ibn Maryam (piuh) is not just one prophet or messenger among others. He is a revelation coming from Allah.

The Deeds of Al-Masih Isa ibn Maryam (piuh)

Al-Masih Isa ibn Maryam (piuh) is the only one whose healing miracles are enumerated in the Honored Quran[35]:

Al-Mā'idah 5:110

> 110 Allah said: "O Isa ibn Maryam, remember My favor to you and your mother .... as you create—by My permission—something out of clay that looks like a bird—by My permission. Then you breathe spirit into it, and it becomes a bird—by My permission. You heal the man born blind and the leper—by My permission, and you bring back the dead—by My permission."

'Āli 'Imrān 3:49a

> 49a "As a messenger for the Children of Israel, I came to you by a sign from your Lord: I create for you something out of clay that looks like a bird. Then I breathe spirit into it and it becomes a bird—by Allah's permission. I heal the blind and the leper and bring back the dead—by Allah's permission. And I prophesy what you eat and what you accumulate in your houses. Indeed, you have a sign in all this—if you believe."

These ayat tells us that Al-Masih Isa ibn Maryam (piuh) can create.[36] According to Surah Al-Ḥajj 22:73, no one can create—not even a fly. Interestingly enough, birds are much bigger than flies! Have you ever wondered how Al-Masih Isa ibn Maryam (piuh) can do that?

Then it is said that Al-Masih Isa ibn Maryam (piuh) heals the sick. In ancient times, leprosy was considered a curse. Al-Masih Isa ibn Maryam (piuh) performs much more than a physical miracle. By healing such a horrendous sickness, he takes away the curse. More than that, he restores the honor of the lepers by reintegrating them into normal society. The same may be said about blindness, symbolic of hopelessness and lack of orientation. Al-Masih Isa ibn Maryam (piuh) can open the eyes of the blind.

---

35 *Yubri'*.

36 *Yaḫluq*.

Let us continue. Al-Masih Isa ibn Maryam (piuh) is the only one to resurrect the dead.[37] Furthermore, the words of Al-Masih Isa ibn Maryam (piuh) are different from those of all others, and he is the only one who knows the unseen and reveals what is done in secret ("what you eat and what you store up").

Finally, Al-Masih Isa ibn Maryam (piuh) is the only one to allow[38] forbidden things:

'Āli 'Imrān 3:50

> 50 (I, Isa, come) to confirm the Taurat revealed before me and to make lawful some of it that was made forbidden. I come to you with a sign from your Lord. So, fear Allah and obey me!

As we know, Allah's Words cannot be changed:

Yūnus 10:64

> 64 Good news for them in the present life and in the Hereafter! There cannot be any change in the words of Allah. This is indeed the supreme felicity.

That is why it is hard to admit that Al-Masih Isa ibn Maryam (piuh) permitted anything previously forbidden. On the contrary, he "confirmed the Taurat revealed before him":

Injil, Gospel of Matthew 5:17-19

> 17 Do not think I came to abolish the law or the prophets. I did not come to abolish, but to fulfill.
> 18 Indeed, I am telling you: Even if heaven and earth passed away, not one jot or one tittle would disappear from the law until everything is fulfilled.
> 19 Therefore, whoever breaks one of the least of these commandments and teaches to do so will be considered least in the kingdom of heaven; but whoever keeps them and teaches them shall be high-ranked in the kingdom of heaven.

In the verses following this declaration, Al-Masih Isa ibn Maryam (piuh) says that he did not suppress any commands but rather restored their initial meaning. For example, he declared that wrongdoing is *what* we do and *why* we do it. Another example is the sacrificial laws. According to the Honored Injil, Jesus (piuh) went beyond their literal application to

---

37 *Yuhyii.*

38 *Yuḥill.*

their spiritual nature. On the other hand, he rejected all human traditions and interpretations elaborated by Jewish scholars, which contradicted the Honored Taurat. One example:

Injil, Gospel of Matthew 5:43, 44

> 43 You have heard that it was said: "Love your neighbor, hate your enemy."
> 44 But I tell you: "Love your enemies, bless those who curse you, do good to those who hate you, and pray for those who abuse and persecute you."

Who Al-Masih Isa ibn Maryam (piuh) Really Is

Neither the Honored Injil nor the Honored Quran allow us to consider Al-Masih Isa ibn Maryam (piuh) as the *physical* son of Allah. At the same time, both Scriptures attest to his divine origin. The oriental concept of "Son of Allah" can best be rendered by *min Allah* (from Allah), which is well attested in the Honored Quran:

- *Raḥmat*^{un} *min-nā*: "Mercy [coming] from Us" (Maryam 19:21)
- *Rūḥ*^{un} *min-hu, rūḥ min-nā*: "Spirit [coming] from Him" and "spirit from Us" (An-Nisā' 4: 171; Al-Anbiyā' 21:91)
- *Kalimat*^{un} *min-hu*: "Word [coming] from Him" ('Āli 'Imrān 3:45)

Indeed, Al-Masih Isa ibn Maryam (piuh) is the only one "glorious in this world and the world to come" and "one near to Allah" ('Āli 'Imrān 3:45) as well. We also know that:

- He was born without an earthly father
- He was born through Allah's Spirit that was breathed into a woman (Al-Anbiyā' 21:91, At-Taḥrīm 66:12)
- He *is* Allah's Spirit (An-Nisā' 4:171)
- He is not only *called* "Allah's Word," but he *is* Allah's Word (An-Nisā' 4:171)
- He is the expression of the Truth) Maryam 19:34)
- He is a sign for the universe (Al-Anbiyā' 21:91)
- He can create, heal, and restore honor. He gives orientation to the blind and knows the unseen ('Āli 'Imrān 3:49, Al-Mā'idah 5:110)
- He is one of those near to Allah ('Āli 'Imrān 3:45).

Finally, some of the names given to him belong to Allah only:

- *Raḥmat min-hu* – Allah is *ar-Raḥmān* (the Compassionate)
- *Qaul al-Ḥaqq* – Allah is *al-Ḥaqq* (the Truth)[39]
- *Yaḫluq* – Allah is *al Ḫāliq* (the Creator)[40]
- *Yuḥyī* – Allah is *al-Muḥyī* (the Giver of life)[41]

An Apparent Contradiction

But doesn't all this contradict other texts saying that Al-Masih Isa ibn Maryam (piuh) was fully submitted to Allah? It is said in Surah az-Zuḫruf 43:59 and in others that he (piuh) was truly (or only) a servant:

> 59 He was indeed a servant. We granted Our favor to him and made him an example to the children of Israel.

Another observation is that Al-Masih Isa ibn Maryam (piuh) performed miracles, but always "*by Allah's permission*" ('Āli 'Imrān 3:49; Al-Mā'idah 5:110). How can we solve the supposed contradiction between his godly titles (piuh) and his seeming dependency on Allah?

Some argue that Al-Masih Isa ibn Maryam (piuh) has the same divine virtues humans have when they are patient[42], wise[43], rich[44], or right.[45] Moreover, some receive a name at birth that describes some divine attributes, such as Adil, Aziz, or Karim.

However, looking at the list of names given to Al-Masih Isa ibn Maryam (piuh), we identify significant differences:

- The Honored Quran applies these names to Al-Masih Isa ibn Maryam (piuh).
- The names are not just features but a personification of these virtues (expressed by the Arabic use of *al)*.
- Some of these names and achievements cannot be applied to human beings but only to Allah.[46]

39 Al-An'ām 6:62; al-Ḥajj 22:6; Al-Mu'minūn 23:116; An-Nūr 24:25.
40 Al-An'ām 6:102; Ar-Ra'd 13:16; Az-Zumar 39:62; Ġāfir 40:62; Al-Ḥašr 59:24.
41 Al-A'rāf 7:158; Al-Ḥijr 15:23; Ar-Rūm 30:50; Al-Ḥadīd 57:2.
42 *Aṣ-Ṣabūr.*
43 *Al-Ḥakīm.*
44 *Al-Ġanī.*
45 *Al-Ḥaqq.*
46 *Rūḥ Ullah, Muqarrab, Kalimat Ullah, Ayat Ullah, Yaḫlu.*

As sincere seekers of the Truth, we must consider the explanations in the Honored Quran:

An-Nisā' 4:172

> 172 Al-Masih will never disdain to be a servant of Allah, nor will the favored angels. Who disdains His services and is proud, all such will He assemble to Him.

This ayah answers the apparent contradiction. It states that Al-Masih Isa ibn Maryam (piuh) *became* a servant of Allah, which suggests that he previously had a higher status.

Also applied to the angels, "not disdaining to be at Allah's service" implies a voluntary act that is the fruit of the decision to humble himself, which can only be done of one's own free will. The verb translated as "to disdain" means "to refuse pride."

That is what Al-Masih Isa ibn Maryam (piuh) chose, which is the opposite of Iblīs' choice to rebel against Allah's authority. Al-Masih demonstrated an exemplary spirit of humility, and his submission to Allah opposed the pride of Iblīs.

All this happened according to Allah's plan long before Al-Masih Isa ibn Maryam's birth. Al-Masih Isa ibn Maryam (piuh) decided to become a servant when he was in high esteem in the world above, which explains why everything he did, while he was on earth, was done in agreement with Allah. That is why he became a servant and, as such, had to ask for consent to perform miracles.

Maryam 19:21

> 21 He (the angel) said, "So shall it be; your Lord says, 'This is something easy for Me to make him a sign for mankind and a mercy from Us. It is a matter decreed.'"

The One Who Says: "Follow Me!" and "Obey Me!"

Finally, the Honored Quran gives the unique command to follow and obey Al-Masih Isa ibn Maryam (piuh):

Az-Zuḫruf 43:61

> 61 And it is a sure sign of the Hour. Therefore, do not be doubtful and follow me! That is a right way.

The construction allows another possible translation: “And indeed, *he* will be knowledge of the Hour. Therefore, be resolute and follow me! That is the Right Way.” If it is so, the one mentioned with “he” would be Al-Masih Isa ibn Maryam (piuh) (according to the context), and “me” would be someone who speaks in the first person. Another text sheds some light on the subject:

Āli ‘Imrān 3:50, 51

> 50 (I, Isa, come) to confirm the Taurat revealed before me and to make lawful some of it that was made forbidden. I come to you with a sign from your Lord. So, fear Allah and obey me!
> 51 Indeed Allah is my Lord and your Lord. Therefore, serve Him. That is a right way.

At first glance, the identification of the one who pronounces the invitation to follow him seems ambiguous. Yet, the ayat before (45-49) and after (52) refer to Al-Masih Isa ibn Maryam (piuh), and they repeat the surah previously quoted in Az-Zuḫruf 43:61, 63, 64:

> 61 And it is a sure sign of the Hour. Therefore, do not be doubtful and follow me! That is a right way.
> 63 And when Isa came through the clear evidence, he said: “Truly, I come to you through wisdom, and clarify some things about which you disagree. Therefore, fear Allah and obey me!
> 64 Surely Allah is my Lord and your Lord. Therefore, serve Him! That is a right way.”

The comparison between these two texts (Surah 3:51, 52 and 43:61, 63, 64) deserves our full attention:

- A brief intermediary separates the Ayat 43:61 and 43:63, 64:

  43:62 “And Satan shall not keep you away. Surely, he is a clear enemy to you”

- Both texts (Ayat 61 and 64) form a unit:

  43:61 “Follow me! That is a right way”
  43:64 “Serve Him! That is a right way”

- The content of Ayat 63 and 64 harmonizes with the structure of Ayat 61:

  43:61 “Therefore, do not be doubtful and follow me! That is a right way”

43:63	"Therefore, fear Allah and obey me!"
43:64	"That is a right way"

- Consequently, Ayat 63 should be understood as the continuation of the train of thought in Ayat 61.
- The wording of Surah 'Āli 'Imrān 3:50 and 51 corresponds to Al-Masih's invitation in 43:63 to fear Allah:

3:50	"Fear Allah!"
43:63	"Fear Allah!"

- The content of Ayat 63 and 64 harmonizes with the structure of 61:

43:61	"Follow me! That is a right way"
43:63	"Obey me!"
43:64	"Allah is my Lord and yours. Serve Him! That is a right way"

- Meanwhile, Ayah 51 clearly specifies that we should follow Jesus (piuh):

3:51	"Allah is my Lord and yours. Serve Him! That is a right way"

- The Ayat before (45-49) and after (52) the above ayat from Surah 'Āli 'Imrān refer to Al-Masih Isa ibn Maryam (piuh). In Surah Az-Zuẖruf 43, the person referred to before (Ayat 59 and 60) the above ayat is Al-Masih Isa ibn Maryam (piuh).

Therefore, the parallels between the two texts cannot be denied. In both cases, the context introduces Al-Masih Isa ibn Maryam (piuh) as the one who tells us to follow and obey him.

This fact eliminates any doubt that Al-Masih Isa ibn Maryam (piuh) is the one whom the Honored Quran asks us to follow and whom we must obey.

> "Al-Masih Isa ibn Maryam (piuh) is the one whom the Honored Quran asks us to follow and obey."

Moreover, as I emphasized previously, Al-Masih Isa ibn Maryam (piuh) is the only one who is called an "eyewitness on the Day of Resurrection" (An-Nisā' 4:159). Therefore, his indication to the title "eyewitness" in connection with the knowledge "of the hour" is consistent with Az-Zuẖruf 43:61.

Conclusion of Chapter 5

To conclude, let us appreciate the importance of being guided on or into the Right Way. To do so, remember when you entered a big city for the first time without knowing the way to your destination. You had several options:

- Driving around until you accidentally found the right street
- Getting a map of the city or a GPS connection
- Asking a local for help; the best option being to contact a taxi driver and let him drive you
- Or you could have called your friend to pick you up where you were

This explains in a simple but accurate way what the Right Way to Allah is:

- Al-Masih Isa ibn Maryam (piuh) invites us to follow him (and "this is the right way"). He can do it because he knows the way well. Indeed, as "word, spirit, and mercy coming from Allah," he has come to us to lead us to the safe goal (which eventually is Paradise).
- Unfortunately, many who claim to follow Al-Masih Isa ibn Maryam (piuh) have deviated from the Right Way (see Chapter 1 in this book).
- Therefore, it is essential not so much to get instruction from others but from the Honored Bible (Taurat, Zabur, and Injil) called "guidance for people" (Al-Baqarah 2:2; Al-Mā'idah 5:46; Al-Aḥqāf 46:30; cf. pp. 71, 72 in this book).
- One may compare the Honored Bible with a roadmap showing us how to follow Al-Masih Isa ibn Maryam (piuh) correctly and who his Bible-oriented followers are.
- That allows us to reach the ultimate goal: eternal bliss in Allah's Paradise.

Some Verses from the Honored Bible

Related to Chapter 5

The following texts illustrate the parallels between the allusions made by Al-Masih Isa ibn Maryam (piuh) in the Honored Quran and by Jesus (piuh) in the Honored Injil, limiting ourselves mainly to the Gospel of John. I leave to you the pleasure of discovering more during your studies.

What Jesus (piuh) Means to Us

Injil, Gospel of John 1:29

29 The next day, he (John the Baptist) saw Jesus approach him and said: "Look, this is the lamb of God who takes away the sin of the world!"

Injil, Gospel of John 3:16, 17

16 God has loved the world. He has sent his only representative ("son") so that everyone who believes in him will not die but have eternal life.
17 Indeed, God has not sent his "son" to condemn the world but for the world to be saved through him.

What Jesus (piuh) Can Do

Injil, Gospel of John 5:8, 9a

8 "Stand up!" Jesus said, "Take your bed and start walking!"
9a Immediately healed, the man took his bed and walked.

Injil, Gospel of John 9:25

25 He [the healed blind man] replied, "Is he a sinner? I don't know! But I know I was blind, and now I can see."

Injil, Gospel of John 20:30, 31
[30] Jesus performed many other signs in the presence of his disciples, which are not recorded in this book.
[31] We have described them so that you believe that Jesus is the Messiah, the "son of God" and that by believing, you have life in his name.

What Jesus (piuh) Has Promised

Injil, Gospel of John 4:29
[29] Come here and see someone who has told me everything I've done! Could it be that he is the Messiah?

Injil, Gospel of John 5:24
[24] I can assure you: Whoever hears my word and believes in the one who sent me has eternal life and will not be sentenced. He has already passed from death to life.

Injil, Gospel of John 6:35
[35] I am the bread of life. Whoever comes to me will never be hungry again, and whoever trusts me will never be thirsty again.

Injil, Gospel of John 7:38, 46
[38] Whoever trusts me, as the Scripture says, living water will flow from him.
[46] The guards replied: "No one has ever spoken like this man."

Injil, Gospel of John 10:11, 14, 15, 27, 28
[11] I am the good shepherd who gives his life for his sheep.
[14] I am the good shepherd. I know my sheep, and they know me,
[15] Just as the "Father" knows me, I know Him, and I give my life for my sheep.
[27] My sheep hear my voice. I know them, and they follow me.
[28] I give them eternal life. They will never perish, and nobody can tear them from my hand.

Injil, Gospel of John 11:25, 26

25 I am the resurrection and the life. Whoever trusts in me will live, even if he dies.

26 Everyone who lives and trusts in me will not die. Do you believe it?

Injil, Gospel of John 14:1, 3, 6, 27

1 Don't be troubled! Believe in God and in me.

3 I will prepare a place for you, return, and take you with me so you can be where I am.

6 I am the way, the truth, and the life. Only through me can you reach the Father.

27 I leave you peace; I give you my peace, not as the world gives. Your heart should not be troubled nor frightened.

The Voluntary Humiliation of Jesus (piuh)

Injil, Gospel of Matthew 24:36

36 Concerning the day and the hour, no one knows them, not even the angels of heaven, the "son," but only the "Father."

Injil, Gospel of John 5:19

19 Truly, I tell you that the "son" cannot do anything by himself except what he sees the "Father" do. All that the "Father" does, the "Son" does it too.

Injil, Epistle of Paul to the Philippians 2:5-8

5 May your mind follow Jesus Christ's example:

6 He who is divine by nature did not consider equality with God as something to be preserved by all means,

7 But he gave it all up, taking the nature of a servant and becoming like a human. Having appeared as a man,

8 He humbled himself, showing himself obedient to the point of death, even death on the cross.

Also Consider

Jesus (piuh) satisfies all needs:

- *Metaphysical*: John 1: He reveals Allah to intellectuals.
- *Familial*: John 2: He contributes to the success of a wedding party.
- *Intellectual*: John 3: He reveals salvation to a religious scholar.
- *Emotional*: John 4: He heals the emotional wounds of a victim of abuse.
- *Physical*: John 5: He heals a hopeless man.

Jesus (piuh) gives to those who:

- *Are hungry*: John 6: He is the bread of life.
- *Are thirsty*: John 7: He is the water of life.
- *Have been dishonored*: John 8: He rehabilitates a fallen woman.
- *Are disoriented*: John 9: He heals a blind man.
- *Are weak*: John 10: He identifies himself with a good shepherd.
- *Are grieving*: John 11: He gives life back to a deceased friend and comforts his relatives.

Closing Words

With this book, I have tried to give the spiritual descendants of Ibrahim (pbuh) some clues, helping them find common ground—or at least come closer to each other. May this publication—*Inshā' Allah*—contribute to peace among them!

Some of our discoveries about the Honored Quran may differ from general interpretation at several points, for instance:

- The "Guidance" presented in the Honored Quran refers to the Honored Bible (whereas it does not mean that no other book can be a guide).
- Al-Masih Isa ibn Maryam (piuh) is the only one named "a mercy originating from Allah" and the only one referred to by name to say: "Follow me!" Even though others may be called "a mercy," only one (Jesus) originates from Allah and invites us to follow him.
- All interpretations presented in this book are grounded in the Honored Quran. Differing opinions might be based on the *Hadiths* (traditions) and on some *mufassirūn* (exegetes) but not on the Honored Quran.
- These new interpretations allow you to look at the Honored Bible and at Al-Masih Isa ibn Maryam (piuh) with different eyes and in a way that builds a bridge toward Christianity.

> "All interpretations presented in this book are grounded in the Honored Quran."

Will you join me in tearing down the dividing walls and building bridges from their stones? Let us study the Honored Quran and the ayat cited in this book together. Let us not disregard the texts about Al-Masih Isa ibn Maryam (piuh). They invite us not to remain among the doubters but to ask those who have read the Scriptures beforehand, as it is said in Yūnus 10:94:

> 94 If you have any doubt concerning what We have sent down to you, ask those who read the Book before you. The Truth comes from your Lord. Therefore, do not be among those who doubt.

I have written this book as a humble contribution to the effort to bring believers of all faiths to a common ground. I hope that it has helped you on your spiritual journey Inshā Allah; I pray that you will ponder the insights that are new to you and incorporate them into your life.

As you finish reading these pages, it is your turn to widen your horizon and continue searching! Allah is pleased with the seekers of the Truth!

Al-Baqarah 2:186

186 When my servants ask you about Me, tell them I am near. I answer the invocation of the supplicant who calls Me. Therefore, let them hear My call and trust Me so they might be rightly guided.

Qaf 50:16

16 We have created man and know what his soul whispers to him, and We are closer to him than his jugular vein.

Therefore, my sincere prayer is that Allah may bless you abundantly in your study of the Sacred Books until you and I someday enjoy what Allah has prepared for all those who walk in the way of our Ibrahim (pbuh), as the Honored Quran says:

'Āli 'Imrān 3:107

107 But as for those whose faces will turn white, they will be within Allah's mercy. They will abide therein eternally.

Maryam 19:61

61 Up there are gardens of perpetual residence that the Most Merciful has promised His servants in the unseen. Indeed, His promise has always been fulfilled.

An-Nisā' 4:125

125 Who is better in religion than he who fully submits to Allah while doing good and following the state of mind of Ibrahim, the upright in faith? Allah chose him as a friend.

May Allah, the King of kings[47] and all Praiseworthy,[48] bless you in your quest for peace of mind as you meditate upon the answers I have tried to give to fundamental issues. May He be thanked for His mercy. He solves existential concerns that impact our peace of mind, and He heals our relationship with other believers. He decides about our eternal destiny!

Ar-Raḥmān 55:78

78 Blessed be the Name of your Lord, the Lord of Majesty and Glory!

---

47 *Mālik al-Mulk.*

48 *Al-Ḥamīd.*

Bibliography

Al Faruqi, Isma'il R. and Al Faruqi, Lois. *The Cultural Atlas of Islam.* London: Macmillan, 1986.

Ali, Syed Ameer. *The Spirit of Islam; Or, the Life and Teachings of Mohammed.* Emeryville: Andesite, 2015.

Aṭ-Ṭabarī, Abū Jaʿfar Muhammad ibn Jarīr. *Tarīkh al-umam wa al-mulūk, vol. 2.* Beirut: Dar-i Seveydan, 1968.

François Berthier, "L'idéologie politique des Frères Musulmans," *Orient Magazine*, no. 8, 1985.

Cowan, James J. M., ed. *The Hans Wehr Dictionary of Modern Written Arabic*, 4th Edition. Wiesbaden: Harrassowitz, 1979.

Dawood, Joseph Nessim. *The Koran.* London: Penguin Classics, 2004.

Dowling, John. *The History of Romanism.* New York: Edward Walker, 1846.

Firestone, Reuven E. *Journeys in Holy Lands: The Evolution of the Abraham-Ishmael Legends in Islamic Exegesis.* New York: State University of New York Press, 1990.

Gesenius, Wilhelm. *Hebräisches und aramäisches Handwörterbuch.* Berlin, Göttingen, Heidelberg: Springer Verlag, 1962.

Gibbon, Edward. *The Decline and Fall of the Roman Empire, vol. 5.* New York City: 2006.

Goffman, Daniel. *The Ottoman Empire and Early Modern Europe.* Cambridge: University Press, 2002.

Kenyon, Frederic George. *The Bible and Archaeology.* London: G. Harrap / New York: Harper & Row, 1940.

Kirk, George E. *A Short History of the Middle East.* New York City: Barnes & Noble, 2006.

Lanarès, Pierre. *Conscience et liberté,* Vol. 2. Bern: Association Internationale pour la Défense de la Liberté Religieuse, 1975.

Mansi, Ioannes Dominicus. *Sacrorum Conciliorum Nova et Amplissima Collectio, Tomus 23, Capitulum 14.* Venice, 1779.

Mirbt, Carl. *Quellen zur Geschichte des Papsttums und des römischen Katholizismus.* Tübingen: Mohr, 1924.

Mynarek, Hubertus, *Die neue Inquisition.* Marktheidenfeld: Das weisse Pferd, 1999.

Phillips, Gabriela. "Islamic Spain, A Model of Peaceful Coexistence." Chattanooga: Self-published, 2003.

Stavrianos, Leften. *The Balkans Since 1453*, 4th Edition. New York: Holt, Rinehart and Winston, 2008.

Treadgold, Warren. *A History of the Byzantine State and Society*. Stanford: Stanford University Press, 1997.

Treece, Henri. *The Crusades*. London: Orion Publishing, 1962.

Tremp, Kathrin Utz. "Frauen, die der Teufel reitet." ZEIT Geschichte, No. 3, August 26, 2014.

Uhlmann, Peter. *Die Lehrentscheidungen Roms im Licht der Bibel.* Amtzell: Telos Verlag, 1984.

Wensierski, Peter, Franke, Klaus, and Schwarz, Ulrich. "Gottes willige Vollstrecker." *Der Spiegel*, June 1st, 1998.

White, E. G. *The Great Controversy*. Mountain View, CA: Pacific Press Publishing Association, 1911.

Other Works by the Author

The Blessed Feast

'Eid Al-Adhā is the biggest religious festival of the Islamic world, during which millions of animals are slaughtered worldwide to commemorate the death of Ibrahim's son (pbuh).

But what is its real meaning?

With over 600 quotations from the Honored Quran, the author presents Allah's plan for rescuing fallen humanity.

Longing for Paradise

Christians and Muslims share the common hope of better days. Both believe that Al-Masih Isa ibn Maryam (piuh) will soon return.

What are the similarities and differences?

The study includes all main eschatological aspects from the Honored Bible, the Honored Quran, the quranic exegesis (*al-mufassirūn*), and the Islamic Traditions (*Hadiths*) on the signs of the times, Allah's ultimate purpose of history, and how to get prepared.

Quran and Bible—A Comparative Study

Suffering: where does it come from, and why does it happen? Common questions—different answers? What does the Honored Bible say? And what about the Honored Quran?

In eight hours of DVD recordings, with PowerPoint presentations of all quotations, you will discover the cosmic conflict and why you are on earth.

Bible Quran on YouTube, Tiktok and Instagram

Finally, we invite you to subscribe to Sylvain Romain's YouTube channel *Bible Quran* (also on TikTok and Instagram). Posts are weekly. Thank you for following it, posting comments, questions, and suggestions, and forwarding the address to your friends!

TEACH Services, Inc.
PUBLISHING

We invite you to view the complete selection of titles we publish at:
www.TEACHServices.com

We encourage you to write us with your thoughts about this, or any other book we publish at:
info@TEACHServices.com

TEACH Services' titles may be purchased in bulk quantities for educational, fund-raising, business, or promotional use.
bulksales@TEACHServices.com

Finally, if you are interested in seeing your own book in print, please contact us at:
publishing@TEACHServices.com

We are happy to review your manuscript at no charge.